# Dedication

*To John, my husband, my love.*

Since it takes two, I'm glad I have *you*.
For all the parenting years behind us,
and those still to come...God is good!

"Chock-full of useful quotes from experts and everyday parents, this is a grace-infused handbook for Gen Xers navigating the parenting journey."

—MARY E. DEMUTH
Author of *Building the Christian Family You Never Had*

"As a young father, I not only relate to Tricia's message, but I'm very encouraged that there is a fantastic parenting resource for our generation."

—JORDAN RUBIN
Founder of Garden of Life
and author of *The Great Physician's RX for Health and Wellness*

# GENERATION NEXT Parenting

TRICIA GOYER

Multnomah® Publishers *Sisters, Oregon*

GENERATION NEXT PARENTING
published by Multnomah Publishers, Inc.

International Standard Book Number: 1-59052-748-8

Cover design by The DesignWorks Group, Inc.
Cover photography by Steve Gardner, www.shootpw.com
Interior design and typset by Katherine Lloyd, The DESK, Sisters, OR

*Italics* in Scripture references and quoted materials are the author's emphasis.



Printed in the United States of America



Library of Congress Cataloging-in-Publication Data

Goyer, Tricia.
Generation next parenting / Tricia Goyer.
p. cm.
ISBN 1-59052-748-8
1. Parenting--Religious aspects--Christianity. 2. Child rearing--Religious aspects--Christianity.
3. Generation X. I. Title.
BV4529.G69 2006
248.8'45--dc22

2006018152

For information:
MULTNOMAH PUBLISHERS, INC.
601 N. LARCH STREET · SISTERS, OREGON 97759

06 07 08 09 10—10 9 8 7 6 5 4 3 2 1 0

# Table of Contents

# INTRODUCTION

## I Promise You

***I'm sorry, but I'm just thinking of the right words to say....***

**WHEN IN ROME, WHEN IN ROME, 1988, VIRGIN RECORDS (USA)**

Maybe you're like me...

In addition to my roles as a parent and writer, I'm also characterized as a child of the '70s and '80s. While I often can't remember my three-item shopping list at the grocery store, I can sing word-for-word such oldies playing over the loudspeaker as "Eye of the Tiger," "Girls Just Wanna Have Fun," and "Beat It."

Like many of my classmates, I wish I could "do over" my teen years. What a mess they were! And how those years continue to impact me now. Fifteen years ago, I thought the movies *Footloose*, *Pretty in Pink*, and *The Breakfast Club* were the coolest. But now, watching them as an adult, I realize they teach an immorality I don't want passed to my kids. (What *was* I thinking?)

I also want more for my kids than what I had. Better family connections. A great love for God. And numerous social and educational opportunities that will not only make their childhood great, but will also mold my kids into productive citizens and awesome servants for God. Is that too much to ask?

You may wonder how this book will differ from many of the parenting books out there. For one, I'm not the head of any parenting organization, nor do I have a national radio broadcast. I don't have a degree in psychology, child development, or anything useful like that.

I'm a young mom (or at least I think so) who graduated from high school in 1989. I wrote a book called *Life Interrupted: The Scoop on Being a Young Mom* (Zondervan, 2004). I've also been writing articles for national magazines about kids and parenting for the last ten years. The best part about writing parenting articles is that I can look around, consider my biggest struggles as a parent, and then interview experts for solutions. How cool is that?

## What This Book Is About

This book won't be about "how to fix your life and your kids." Instead, the idea emerged after I noticed how different I was from parents in the generations before me. I'm one of those people who wants to do it all—find God's purpose for my life, impact my community, support my spouse, and provide my children every opportunity available to them.

I'm not content working nine to five *just* to bring home a paycheck. I hate the thought of not being actively involved in my kids' lives. The dozens of parenting books on my bookshelves confirm I'm committed to doing it right. (If only I had time to read them!)

This book is for you. For *us*. To provide a little hope, a few facts about our generation of parents, and a lot of encouragement to turn to God on this journey.

If you were born between 1961 and 1981, maybe you can relate. We're called Generation X, and to me the X stands for:

**eX-cellent people, eX-celling to our potential,
and eX-hausted most of the time!**

We want to do it all, be it all, and parent as well as possible. And according to the experts who study society, the two words that describe our beliefs are *authentic* and *relationships*. We don't want anyone to put on a show for us. We want the real deal. And, of course, what matters most to us is *people*.

Oh yeah, and one more characteristic of our generation: We are very serious parents. It's true! Just ask the experts, or take a look at what we expect from our children and ourselves. In truth, we're all a little more alike than you might imagine.

## My Take On It

"There are way too many choices and distractions in our lives. Technology keeps us from talking to each other and busy schedules mean we rarely eat together unless it's in the car."

**—Michelle H., Arizona**
**Born in 1967, mother of two**

"I feel Gen X parents are constantly comparing ourselves and our children with our friends and their offspring. Not in a 'keeping up with the Joneses' kind of way, but because we're insecure about the job we're doing as parents. I find myself constantly questioning: Am I providing enough intellectual stimulation for my child? Is my daughter getting enough socialization? Should she have reached x, y, or z milestone by now? Basically, am I really doing a good job? And exactly what does a good job of parenting look like?"

**—Michelle, New Jersey**
**Born in 1968, mother of one**

We're not driven to give our kids the best, but to give them everything. We buy more and more stuff in the hopes it makes us good parents. In order to pay for this stuff, we work harder and harder, which takes time away from our families, which increases the immense load of guilt. Every night of the week is filled with soccer, ballet, piano, tutoring, and we still don't feel like we are giving our kids enough opportunities, so we try harder, and in the end we feel empty, unfulfilled."

**—Heidi, Minnesota**
**Born in 1975, mother of two**

*

## More About Us

There are plenty of reasons Gen Xers turned out the way we did. Here are some biggies:

- More of our moms entered the workforce.
- More of our parents divorced.
- Either we were sexually promiscuous or we had friends who were.
- When it came to drugs and alcohol, it was pretty easy to get our hands on them.
- We don't remember prayer as a part of school.
- We do remember every episode of *The Cosby Show*, and oftentimes we related more to that family than our own.
- We remember the first video we saw on MTV, and musicians like Bruce Springsteen, Tiffany, and Billy Idol were our, uh, idols.

Of course, I could go on, but this book wasn't written just to reminisce about "the good ol' days." It's about understanding who we are as a generation and why we became the parents we are today. More than that, it's about taking our good qualities...and discovering how to parent better, for God's glory.

But before we get into the actual chapters, I'm going to end this introduction with a few more facts. The more I read about Gen Xers and the more I interview other young parents, the more I realize we share many of the same desires, hopes, and dreams. We also experience similar struggles in parenting. Who would have thought?

## The Bottom Line

While you may see yourself in the descriptions above, it does little good if you can't find a solution. The pages that follow will cover topics that are important to Gen Xers. And along with these helps, my major goal is to offer *hope*.

# The FACTS

- Gen Xers consist of 41 million Americans born between 1961 and 1981, plus the 3 million more in that age group who have immigrated here.
- Gen Xers are serious about life. We don't take life as it comes, but give great consideration to critical decisions about our present and future. When it comes to parenting, we want to do it right. We take parenting seriously because we remember the latchkey existence with too much free time and too little parental involvement, and we want to give our kids more.
- Gen Xers are stressed out. We want to do it all...now. And when we do, we find ourselves overwhelmed—work, family, and the techno-stress that 24/7 communication such as cell phones, e-mail, and instant messaging has brought about. We've bought into following our dreams and finding our purpose. Yet we struggle to balance kids, ministry, work, and service. (We love to volunteer, to give, to help, to make a difference!)
- Gen Xers are self-reliant yet highly spiritual. We're skeptical, yet eager to apply what we do believe to our everyday lives. We're realistic, not idealistic. Our faith has to be truly lived-out or we don't buy into it.
- According to a recent George Barna study, only 28 percent of Gen Xers (ages 20–37) attend church compared to 51 percent of Builders (58+). Yet a **Newsweek** article recently suggested that "81 percent of Gen X mothers and 78 percent of fathers say they plan eventually to send their young child to Sunday school or some other kind of religious training."
- Because of the loneliness and alienation of splintered family attachments, "experts" have claimed that the strongest desire of Gen Xers is acceptance and belonging. Unfortunately, as parents, we don't often find the companionship and acceptance we long for. Sometimes we feel alone, as if we're the only ones dealing with these parenting struggles.
- Gen Xers believe in giving the best to our kids, we really do. Yet we question if we're doing it right—or if we can do it at all. If we don't follow in our parents' parenting footsteps, is something wrong with us? Is it okay to do it our own way?

God placed us in a specific generation *as children* in order for us to become a generation *of parents* designed to fulfill His chosen purposes. In the crazy way God works, Generation X has been chosen to parent the *next generation* of powerful men and women of God!

God knows what He's doing after all, giving us these kids during this time in history. We also need to remember that He hasn't left us to do this job alone. While you will find many helpful suggestions in the pages to come, my ultimate hope is that you'll build a deeper connection with God. He can provide far more parenting help and guidance than any book ever could.

## The Problem

According to a 2003 survey of 3,020 parents, twice as many Gen X mothers as boomer mothers spent more than twelve hours a day attending to child-rearing and household responsibilities. Roughly half of Gen X fathers devoted three to six hours a day to domesticity. Only 39 percent of baby boomer dads could say the same.

**Who would have guessed Gen Xers—the so-called cynical drifters of the 1980s—would end up complaining about too little time with their children?**

Gen Xers are great parents who provide tons of time with their kids. Yet the problems arise when:

- We're overwhelmed, wanting to give our children everything **now**.
- We're tired of trying to do **too much**.
- We're unfocused, wanting our children to experience **everything**.
- We're **on our own**—many times living hundreds or thousands of miles from family support.
- We're curious about spiritual matters, but often **don't know how to connect**.

## Final Note

One more thing I want to mention is the use of song lyrics from the 1970s and '80s in the text. Do I quote these singers and groups because they're upstanding people who have answers? Not at all. I quote them because their music defined our times. I quote them because they reveal our questions. Within these lyrics lie the thoughts, longings, hopes, and confusion of an entire generation.

And within God's holy Word are the answers we sought then and still seek now.

# 1 Time After Time

## Depending on God

***If you're lost you can look—and you will find me....***

—Cyndi Lauper, *She's So Unusual*, 1983, Legacy Recordings

Have you ever wondered why, out of all times in history, God chose to place us into an age bracket referred to as "Generation X"?

As much as I love history (I've written four novels set during World War II), I'm thankful to live in this age of computers, coffee, and cell phones. In fact, even as I write these words I'm sitting in an Internet café drinking my double-shot, sugar-free mocha frappe, trying to collect my thoughts while an espresso machine whirs in the background.

How did God know I'd love so many things about living in this era, like watching dramatic, high-budget films like *Lord of the Rings*, having e-pen-pals in places like Austria and Aruba, and being able to check e-mail on my camera phone even when I'm miles from home?

Of course, in this day and age there are also challenges unique to our generation when it comes to raising kids. In talking with Gen X parents and reading through the dozens of surveys e-mailed to me, I've become aware of some unique worries that our parents never considered, such as:

- media's effect on young children
- how much Nintendo is too much
- how to fulfill our life's calling while also raising kids

And those are just some of the minor issues—let's not forget the more serious downward spiral of morality in America. If you're like me, sometimes you may wonder just what type of world you've birthed your child into.

But it helps to remember that none of these changes in society are a surprise to God. He's not surprised by Hollywood or Supreme Court decisions. He doesn't shrug His shoulders in bewilderment over MTV or the ACLU. In fact, God not only knew what the world would look like in the 1980s, 1990s, 2000s; *He knew our place in it.*

> From one man he made every nation of men, that they should inhabit the whole earth; and *he determined the times set for them and the exact places where they should live.* God did this so that men would seek him and perhaps reach out for him and find him, though he is not far from each one of us. (Acts 17:26–27)

One of my favorite techniques for studying the Bible is to check out the Greek/Hebrew definition in the study Bible on my computer. This gives me a better sense of the meaning behind the biblical writers' words.

For example, the word *determined* in verse 26 means "He *arranged* the set and proper times." God not only picked the era in which we were born; He arranged our place in it for a reason.

The next verse goes on to say, "God did this so that men would *seek* him." The word *seek* here means more than the childhood game of hide-and-seek. In fact, another definition for *seek* is "require"—as in "God did this so that men would *require* him and perhaps reach out for him and find him."

Here's My Take On It: God placed us parents in this time in history because no matter how bright, or skilled, or committed we are (and our generation is all of these things), achieving success as parents means requiring His involvement in our daily lives.

Although I would never directly credit one of my favorite '80s singers, Cyndi Lauper, with drawing me closer to God, I do imagine the chorus from her song "Time After Time" as words God might use to speak to our generation.

God was aware of the vicious cycles we'd face. He understood we'd be overwhelmed and in need of direction. He knew, as Lauper sings, that we'd sometimes be lost and sometimes feel like we're falling.

He also realized that in order for us to be all we can and to raise children who serve Him, we would be *required* to seek and depend on Him. We would require Him... time after time.

> There is a mysterious cycle in human events. To some generation much is given. Of other generations much is expected. This generation has a rendezvous with destiny.
>
> **—Franklin Delano Roosevelt, 1936**

After all, being a generation of parents in a high-speed and morally confused world doesn't allow for anything less.

## Say You, Say Me

***Say it together naturally....***

**—Lionel Richie, Dancing on the Ceiling, 1985, Motown Records**

One of the main characteristics of Generation X parents is that we're very relational. People matter. I don't know about you, but I absorb a lot of parenting information during the day—TV, parenting magazines, Dr. Phil—yet they don't really become concrete in my thinking until I discuss these ideas with a friend.

Just last night, I took a walk with my friend, Tara. Although we didn't go more than a few miles, we conversed on activities we've signed our kids up for, ways to make our hubbies feel good (give his arm muscles a good squeeze and compliment his strength), and a dozen other topics about home life.

And you know what? Going on that walk not only revved up my body, but it helped me put into words things I've been wanting to work on and change in my life. In fact, I left our time together with new ideas and new hope for the week ahead.

"We all need encouragement," inspirational speaker Florence Littauer once said. "We *can* live without it just as a young tree can live without fertilizer, but unless we receive that warm nurturing, we never reach our full potential, and like the tree left to itself, we seldom bear fruit."

Do you have a friend you can turn to, talk with, or walk with on this parenting journey? Consider asking a friend or your spouse to read *Generation NeXt Parenting* with you and make an appointment in person, over the phone, or via e-mail to share your thoughts. It will give you someone to bounce ideas off of. And if nothing else, you'll discover that perhaps you're not the only one with parenting insecurities, parenting hopes, and parenting dreams.

## My Take On It

"Good friends encourage me as we discuss our struggles and realize we aren't alone. We pray for each other and share our concerns at Bible study. I make time for me by having an occasional girls' night out. Fortunately, my husband supports this."

**—Michelle H., Arizona**
**Born in 1967, mother of two**

"Oh, thank God for providing friends! I have another mom whom I talk with almost every single day. It helps both of us to maintain our sanity. I also have other friends from my hometown (now 3 1/2 hours away) that I can e-mail or IM."

**—Jenn, New York**
**Born in 1972, mother of one**

"My closest friend is my husband, Keith. We talk about everything, and I've never felt insecure or judged. He's my support, my rock, and my confidant. I know I can tell him everything, and he won't think I'm some crazy lady on the edge of life that needs to be medicated!"

**—Katie, Texas**
**Born in 1971, mother of four**

# BONUS MATERIAL

***A Peer Personality is a generation persona recognized and determined by (1) common age location; (2) common beliefs and behavior; and (3) perceived membership in a common generation.*** [1]

## DIFFERENT GENERATIONS LOOK AT LIFE DIFFERENTLY

Every one of us is an individual, with a unique set of attitudes, culture, opinions and personality. All of these combine to give us a unique view of events, and they shape our reactions to circumstances. The way in which we process what is going on around us is known as our "world view," or value system. It's this part of us that determines what is good or bad, normal or weird, right or wrong. This value system is largely in place by the time we reach our teens.[2]

Because of its unique value system, each generation also approaches God in a different way.

The authors of *Mind the Gap!* offer the following information:

***GI:*** Born 1900s to 1920s

***Silent:*** Born 1920s to 1940s

***Boomer:*** Born 1940s to 1960s

***Xer:*** Born 1960s to 1980s

***Millennial:*** Born 1980s to 2000s[3]

## STYLE OF WORSHIP

***GIs:*** Formulaic. Attracted to religious events that are rich with pomp and ornate ceremony.

***Silents:*** Quiet, reverential. "Be still and know that I am God" approach.

***Boomers:*** "It's a Big Message, so spread it in a Big Way." Slick, professional.

***Xers:*** Intimate, nonjudgmental, personally connected with my God.

***Millennials:*** Eager to integrate all the spiritual threads of their lives. Desire to explore other religious traditions.[4]

# 2

# I'M GONNA LIVE FOREVER

## The Heavenly Reality

***Baby, remember my name....***

—IRENE CARA, FAME SOUNDTRACK, 1980, POLYGRAM

While I was growing up, one of my favorite television shows was *The Brady Bunch*—reruns, of course. What a nice family: dad, mom, six kids, maid, dog. They had struggles, for sure, but nothing that couldn't be wrapped up by the end of the episode.

I'm not sure what I imagined life would be like once I became a mother. I have the house, the husband, and the kids. (We've stopped at three...for now.) We even have a dog...*and* a hamster. How's that for being a "real" family?

Yet the reality is there's no Alice—except in my dreams. And instead of only one predicament per daily episode, there's more like two or three...or twenty. Kids arguing. Schoolwork to oversee. Job deadlines. A car on its last leg. My husband's business trips. A sore back from spending too much time at the computer. Twenty extra pounds. Or a call from the neighbor stating my five-year-old son tossed a basket of strawberries through her car window, and she didn't notice until *after* she sat down. (I'd like to know how Mrs. Brady would have handled that!)

Life is not like the TV shows we watched growing up. In reality, people don't act and react through scripted lines, and there's no sappy background music to clue us in to a happy ending right around the corner.

Yet, there *is* something similar between those television sitcoms and real life: *There's a lot more going on behind the scenes than what we see.* TV viewers see a happy family interacting in their living room, but so much more is happening outside our line of vision—like the cameraman intent on getting the right angle, or the lighting director ensuring there are no shadowed faces.

The fact is, we too often miss out on the behind-the-scenes shots. We get so wrapped up in the drama going on around us that we forget about the Director sitting on the sidelines, intent on providing input.

### My Take On It

"I've realized I won't hit 'perfect' this side of heaven. It's so discouraging to be given two or ten steps from a parenting manual that I don't understand how to apply, and then to be told how well the steps work if I'd just do them right and on a consistent basis. There's only one perfect Parent. As for me, I'm realistic about growing and failing and learning."

**—Amy, Georgia**
**Born in 1970, mother of three**

"I honestly don't think God intended for parenting to be as stressful as we make it. I mean, God knew it would be hard because life is, but we put so many unnecessary demands on ourselves. I'm still doing it and probably always will."

**—Jeanette, Nevada**
**Born in 1967, mother of two**

## The Unseen Reality

I can't remember most of the movie *Fame,* except for the girl dancing around in a leotard and legwarmers with these words crying out of the boom box: *"I'm gonna live forever.... Baby, remember my name!"*

The words to Fame were more right-on than we realized. As Christians, we will live forever, make it to heaven, and light up the sky. Our goal as parents is that our kids will, too. It's what we want most. After all, what good would we have accomplished if we raise kids who are successful and beautiful yet never accept Jesus as their Savior? How heartbreaking it would be to see them achieve happiness on earth but never experience the joy of standing before the Father and hearing, "Well done, good and faithful servant."

Yet too often what means the most in light of eternity is often the easiest to forget. Basketball practice and Boy Scouts are scheduled events; Bible reading is not. We wouldn't necessarily say piano lessons and play dates put the squeeze on prayer, but by the end of the day we're thrilled with a simple "Lord, thank You for this day."

Of course, I'm relating this as someone who struggles with these very issues. I want my kids to be awesome Christians. I want to memorize Scripture as a family. I want to worry less about "stuff" and focus more on eternity. I long to put God first in all areas of my home life, but my focus on spiritual practices is wanting...except for one thing that has helped me consistently: attempting to tune in to the behind-the-scenes reality often ignored in the daily drama.

Colossians 3:1–4 says, "Since, then, you have been raised with Christ, set your hearts on things above, where Christ is seated at the right hand of God. Set your minds on things above, not on earthly things. For you died, and your life is now hidden with Christ in God. When Christ, who is your life, appears, then you also will appear with him in glory."

Another way the word *hearts* is translated in the sentence "set your hearts on things above" is the word *affections.* If I dig a little deeper into my

Greek and Hebrew study notes, I see that the word *affections* is not passive; instead, it means "to actively exercise your mind and interest yourself with things above."[5]

While there is a ton of great advice out there about being a godly parent and raising godly kids, there is one thing that works for me daily and without fail. It is focusing my mind—even for three minutes—on heavenly things.

## My Take On It

"I struggle with making time to pray and read my Bible. Quiet times with God, where I read the Bible and prayed for at least thirty minutes a day, pretty much flew out the door with the birth of my first child."

**—Melanie, Alabama**
**Born in 1970, mother of two**

"I am tired. Worn out. Beat. I know I need to be disciplined in Scripture study, prayer, and eternal focus, but the truth is, I am just too worn out to think. I read the book **Practicing the Presence of God**. I strived to be like Brother Lawrence, always walking in the joy of the Lord. I tried it. But I find it dreadfully difficult to keep my mind focused on the Lord while changing my fifteenth diaper of the day or cleaning applesauce off of the walls (again), while the kids are fighting over which TV show to watch (again). I sit down to pray, read the Bible, or write in my journal, and I either don't know what to say or am just too plain worn out to say it."

**—Michelle H., Ohio**
**Born in 1971, mother of four**

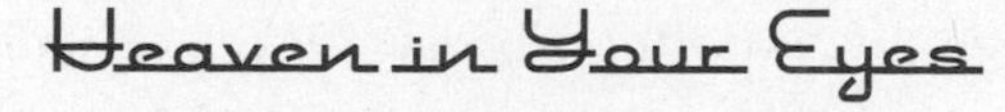

## Heaven in Your Eyes

***It took some time to find the light,***
***but now I realize...***
***I can see the heaven in your eyes.***

LOVERBOY, *BIG ONES*, 1989, COLUMBIA (USA)

Just today my friend Robin sent me a link to a software program perfect for those who spend hours each day on the computer. It's called Stretch Break, and it flashes reminders to stretch up on the screen at regular intervals; it even provides specific stretches to try. It's a great help in reminding me to exercise my body in small ways.

Of course, even more important is exercising my thoughts and setting my heart on things above. For me, this realization happens when I take time to escape with God. To seek Him, remember Him, and ask to be strengthened by Him.

For hundreds of years, Christian seekers have focused their minds on God and called it "meditation." I'm not talking about a Zen-Buddhist thing. In fact, numerous times the Bible speaks of "meditating on the Lord's goodness."

And while Gen Xers long to discover the spiritual disciplines of our ancestors, we also are realistic about what works for *real life*. As parents, most of us don't have a free hour where we can sit and think about the Lord's goodness. That's why I encourage you to try this:

## The Three-Minute Escape

1. Head to a spot in your home where you can find a bit of peace. I like my bed, but a cozy chair would be good, too. Or perhaps a bathroom stall at work. Or a corner in your attic. Even a soundproof booth will do.

2. If possible, shut the door. Crawl under the covers, if you like. Ignore the pounding on the door and the barking dog.

3 Close your eyes and take three cleansing breaths. With each breath, pray a simple prayer such as, "Jesus, make Your heavenly realm real to me at this moment."

4 Imagine God seated on His throne. Picture His loving gaze. Conjure your favorite images of heaven from the Bible. Consider heaven as real as the world around you. In fact, think of it as the part of the "behind the scenes" you can't see, with the Director overseeing it all.

5 Remember God's power and goodness. Thank Him for His love. Thank Him that the reality of heaven is even more than what you can imagine.

6 Offer your worries and concerns to Him. Imagine casting them to His feet.

7 Thank God for your weaknesses, and pray for His strength to become strong in you. Ask Him for this strength. "Lord, I'm too weak. I can't handle these bills, these cranky kids, this mounting deadline for work. I need You to be strong through me."

8 Feel His presence as He meets you there. Breathe in His peace.

9 If you'd like, keep note cards close by with Scripture passages. Whisper them as a prayer. "But seek first his kingdom and his righteousness, and all these things will be given to you as well" (Matthew 6:33).

10 Return to life three minutes later, refreshed and strengthened by your Lord.

I can't say I take a three-minute escape on a daily basis. There are days when I'm constantly on the go and simply unable to sneak away. Other times I find myself curled up in my bed for a few minutes every hour!

And as I meditate on heavenly places, I especially like to imagine the side of the throne where I spot Jesus bringing my needs before God. After all,

Romans 8:34 says, "Christ Jesus, who died—more than that, who was raised to life—is at the right hand of God and is also interceding for us."

I like the image of Jesus raising His hand to get His Father's attention: "Uh, God, don't forget Tricia down there. She's having a challenging day. Let's show her Our love in a special way as she takes time to turn her heart toward heaven."

Taking this time and focusing on this spiritual "reality" helps me, strengthens me, refreshes me. And because of it I *am* a better person and a better mom.

> The man who gazes upon and contemplates day by day the face of the Lord Jesus Christ, and who has caught the glow of the reality that the Lord is not a theory but an indwelling power and force in his life, is as a mirror reflecting the glory of the Lord.
>
> **—Alan Redpath**

## Eye in the Sky

***...looking at you***

***ALAN PARSONS PROJECT, BEST OF THE ALAN PARSONS PROJECT, 1983, ARISTA RECORDS (USA)***

One of my friends, Kim, shared in Sunday school about her daughter's fascination with the clouds.

"Sometimes when we're driving," Kim says, "Ellie will point to the sky and say, 'I wonder if *those* are the clouds Jesus will come back on?'"

Another friend, Car (pronounced *Care*), has a son who loves pointing out beautiful sunrises or sunsets: "Look, Mom. Look at what God painted in the sky just for us!'

"Now all our family takes turns saying it at different times to cheer each other up," Car says. "God loves us all enough to display an original work of art every now and then."

When children are young, it's easy for them to imagine heaven touching down on earth. They're in awe of the world and the beauty around them, and have no hesitation in giving the glory to God.

As parents, it's our job to encourage this. Help your children see God's presence in day-to-day life as you go for walks, drive around in the car, or even play in the yard. Remind your kids when they accept Jesus as their Savior they too will live forever, make it to heaven, and light up the sky. In fact, this is the ultimate *Fame* they can look forward to.

## My Take On It

"With my first child it felt really weird to say things like, 'Look at the sunset! Thank You, God, for this beautiful sky.' It felt forced. But the more I did it, and the more I saw my daughter do it with an excited heart, the more real it became for me.

"I've also moved past the suggested 'Sunday school phrases' to things that are more natural. Like sharing what stirs within me when I look at the ocean—how big God seems when I consider how I can't even see the end of the Gulf water in front of me.

"Watching my little ones nod and stare out over the ocean waves, thinking about how big God is and smiling, makes me desire even more to share little moments of truth."

**—Amy, Georgia**
**Born in 1970, mother of three**

# BONUS MATERIAL

## WHICH OF THESE GEN XERS WOULD YOU WANT TO BE YOUR PARENT?

Born in 1964...

Nicholas Cage, actor, *Raising Arizona*

Teri Hatcher, actress, *Desperate Housewives*

Keanu Reeves, actor, *The Matrix*

Born in 1965...

David Robinson, NBA forward

Sarah Jessica Parker, actress, *Sex and the City*

Shania Twain, country singer

Born in 1966...

Mike Tyson, boxer

Cindy Crawford, model

Halle Berry, actress, *X-Men*

Born in 1967...

Julia Roberts, actress, *Pretty Woman*

Faith Hill, singer

Tim McGraw, singer

Born in 1968...

Mary Lou Retton, gymnast, 1984 Olympic gold medalist

Will Smith, rapper/actor, *Men in Black*

Cuba Gooding Jr., actor, *Radio*

Born in 1969...

Jennifer Aniston, actor, *Friends*

Emmitt Smith, NFL running back

Renee Zellweger, actress, *Bridget Jones's Diary*

Born in 1970...

M. Night Shyamalan, filmmaker, *The Sixth Sense*

Mariah Carey, pop singer

Kirk Cameron, actor

Born in 1971...

Lance Armstrong, cyclist, seven-time Tour de France winner

Winona Ryder, actress, *Edward Scissorhands*

Luke Wilson, actor, *The Royal Tenenbaums*

Born in 1972...

Ben Affleck, actor, *Pearl Harbor*

Cameron Diaz, actress, *There's Something About Mary*

Monica Lewinsky, former White House intern

Born in 1973...

Rose McGowan, actress, *Charmed*

Monica Seles, tennis player

Ichiro Suzuki, Major League baseball outfielder

Born in 1974...

Leonardo Di Caprio, actor, *Titanic*

Jewel, singer

Kate Moss, supermodel

Born in 1975...

Tiger Woods, golfer

Drew Barrymore, actress, *E.T.*

Kate Winslet, actress, *Titanic*

Born in 1976...

Candace Cameron, actress, *Full House*

Alicia Silverstone, actress, *Clueless*

Reese Witherspoon, actress, *Legally Blonde*

Born in 1977...

Brittany Murphy, actress, *Girl, Interrupted*

Peja Stojakovic, NBA guard, Sacramento Kings

Maggie Gyllenhall, actress, *Mona Lisa Smile*

Born in 1978...

Ashton Kutcher, actor, *Just Married*

Usher Raymond, singer

Katie Holmes, actress, *Dawson's Creek*

Born in 1979...

Norah Jones, musician/singer

Kate Hudson, actress, *Raising Helen*

Heath Ledger, actor, *A Knight's Tale*

*Did you pick one? Which character traits helped you make your choice? Which person would you most want your own children to have for a role model?*

# 3 I Don't Know Much

## Parenting Advice Overload

***But I know I love you, that may be all I need to know....***

*Linda Ronstadt with Aaron Neville, Cry Like a Rainstorm, Howl Like the Wind, 1989, Elektra Entertainment*

When was the last time you checked out the parenting section at your local bookstore? Or flipped through one of those *Practical Parenting* magazines that show up in your mailbox? Or signed up for the new video series at church? Or listened to a parenting program on your local Christian radio station? I don't know about you, but sometimes I'm overwhelmed with all the advice.

"Raise children to be missions minded. There is a whole world out there in need of Christ."

"Teach your children to memorize Scripture verses on a daily basis, hiding His word in their hearts."

"Bake homemade cookies with your children and distribute them to your neighbors. We can each be lights for Jesus in our own neighborhood."

"You need to..."

"God calls you to..."

"Our world needs you to..."

The numerous messages can be overwhelming. Yet, I also feel if I don't listen, don't pick up the book, don't pay attention, then I'm a horrible parent. After all, maybe their advice will be the one thing I've been looking for to transform my home and family.

It's all great stuff, it really is. I always glean a few kernels of wisdom from every book I read. But how can we possibly be expected to incorporate it all? The answer, of course, is that we can't—yet we feel guilty for lack of trying.

It's even worse when I'm the one writing the parenting articles, such as "How to Stop Sibling Rivalry," "Ten Ways to Make Chores Exciting," and "Easy Solutions for Picky Eaters." After all, it's easy to write about what we should do. I just call a few experts and ask a few friends for suggestions.

But if the writer of the article (*ahem*) doesn't even have time to follow through on these suggestions, what hope does the rest of the world have?

I could fill the pages of this book with worthwhile ideas (or at least, *I* think they'd be worthwhile), but what good will it do if they never make one iota of difference in your life?

> Xers now have children just beginning to toddle off to school and they watch with the pride borne of being truly hands-on parents. As a result, the parenting "industry" is booming. From prenatal classes to child psychologists, baby stores, and parenting books, the demand is such that it's hard to keep up. Most Xer parents have been on at least one parent course. They don't like taking advice from their parents and are the first generation that has, en masse, not gone running back to mother at some stage in the first year of their child's life.[6]

## My Take On It

"The parenting advice available today is so completely overwhelming! And so much of it is conflicting. It's hard to decide which to choose. To spank or not to spank. To use time out or not. To let them 'cry it out' or not. Then when you try their suggestions and it doesn't work, you start to lose hope. I often wonder what is wrong with my children! Why don't these things work for them? Or what is wrong with me? It makes me feel like I've failed big-time."

**—Lauri, Michigan**
**Born in 1969, mother of four**

"As a Christian, it is difficult to decide what good advice is and what will steer you away from the morals and values you hold. I'm terrified of reading the 'wrong' book. On the flip side, I'm often glad the information is there. When something new pops into my life I need to know everything there is about it and how to deal with it. But in the end, after I've read up on the parenting topic of choice, it's up to me to pray and read His Word to ultimately guide my decision."

**—Abbey, South Dakota**
**Born in 1977, mother of two**

"I think one of the bigger challenges as a parent is that we have to reconcile crappy role-models with an insane desire to be perfect parents, because we don't want our kids to grow up as screwed up as we did and blame us. Thus, we look to the 'experts' to help us define what makes the perfect parent. What drives me nuts, though, is for every expert out there, there is another expert who says exactly the opposite, and there are thousands of them. Sometimes I just wish somebody could tell me how to do it right and know that my kids are going to grow up to be stable, emotionally healthy adults."

**—Heidi, Minnesota**
**Born in 1975, mother of two**

## Good Advice

We all know there is a big difference between reading, hearing, or even writing good advice and incorporating it into our lives. James 1:22 says, "But prove yourselves doers of the word, and not merely hearers who delude themselves" (NASB).

Forming a bad habit is easy. Yet attempting to integrate a positive practice is another story. Maybe it's because we're going about it the wrong way. Gregory A. Boyd, author of *Seeing Is Believing,* says:

> We are being naive and unbiblical if we think that our effort is the primary way we bring about fundamental change in our lives. While willpower plays a role in overcoming behavioral problems, it cannot itself change fundamental aspects of a person's character. For example, willpower alone cannot make an unloving person into a loving person or a depressed person into a joyful person.
>
> Indeed, when it comes to fundamental aspects of a person's character, exhortations to try harder often result in the person pretending he or she is one way when that is not the case. A person can try hard to *act* loving and joyful when he or she is actually unloving and depressed, but a person cannot actually *become* loving and joyful simply by trying to be so.
>
> The fruit of the Spirit is not first and foremost about how we *act*; it is about how we *are.* It is not about our *behavior*; it is about our *heart*, our *soul*, our *innermost disposition.* As such, the fruit of the Spirit is not something we can or should strive to produce by our own effort. The fruit of the Spirit is not a goal we can and must seek to attain. Indeed, it is called the fruit *of the Spirit* precisely because it is the fruit *of the Spirit* and not the product of our own effort.[7]

I don't know about you, but these words were very liberating to me. It's not about hearing great parenting advice and using my willpower to make it happen. Rather, it's about *allowing* the Spirit to work in my life.

We are all familiar with Galatians 5:22–23, "But the fruit of the Spirit is love, joy, peace, patience, kindness, goodness, faithfulness, gentleness and self-control." But too often we forget to read what follows. Galatians 5:25 says, "Since we live by the Spirit, let us keep in step with the Spirit."

I love how this verse is phrased in my Interlinear Bible (wherein each line of the original biblical text—OT Hebrew or NT Greek—is followed by a literal English equivalent):

> If we live in the Spirit, in the Spirit let us also walk.

The word *walk* here has a cool meaning. It means to "march in rank as in the military; to conform to virtue and piety."[8]

Some people believe "living by the Spirit" means flitting from here to there with every wind that blows our way. In fact, the opposite is true. The Spirit leads us in step and rank. Just look around at this amazing world. God *is* the God of precision and orderliness.

For me this means taking time away to read my Bible and pray, then to listen to that still, small voice speaking through my conscience.

In *Seeing Is Believing,* Gregory A. Boyd tells us:

> Each day He wants to make His guidance natural and normal. He is not there to dominate you or take over your personhood. He is there to make you effective as a person. He desires to bring His suggestions to your mind—whether positive or negative—in such a natural way that you hardly realize it.[9]

## My Take On It

"I trust the Spirit to guide me when I'm not sure of the best answer or solution, which is often! Although during the times when I 'walk in step with the Spirit,' I also find myself crying a lot because it's hard to trust and give up control."

**—Michelle H., Arizona**
**Born in 1967, mother of two**

"Walking in the Spirit means walking with an open ear to His voice throughout my days. I try to apply this concept to my parenting journey because I would fail without His input on a daily basis."

**—Cara, Indiana**
**Born in 1974, mother of two**

"Walking in the Spirit means the Holy Spirit's influence is with me on a continuous basis, whether He is counseling me, directing me, protecting me, or letting me walk a bumpy road. I am constantly asking God to help me as a parent. Begging, actually."

**—Rene, Oklahoma**
**Born in 1972, mother of two**

"I'm learning I can't 'apply' walking with God to parenting. It's either a natural outflow of my time with God, or it doesn't happen. It's all about that authenticity thing. If it's not real in my heart, I can't make it real in my parenting, no matter how hard I try."

**—Amy, Georgia**
**Born in 1970, mother of three**

## Daily Guidance

This week, I happened to be reading through the book of Proverbs in my personal Bible study. Here are a few of the verses I highlighted:

> I guide you in the way of wisdom and lead you along straight paths. When you walk, your steps will not be hampered; when you run, you will not stumble. (Proverbs 4:11–12)

> A man's steps are directed by the Lord. How then can anyone understand his own way? (Proverbs 20:24)

> Trust in the Lord with all thine heart; and lean not unto thine own understanding. In all thy ways acknowledge him, and he shall direct thy paths. (Proverbs 3:5–6, KJV)

There is a ton of advice out there, and there will always be. But the steps of righteous people—our steps—are directed by the Lord. As Oswald Chambers says in *My Utmost for His Highest*:

> We can all see God in exceptional things, but it requires the growth of spiritual discipline to see God in every detail. Never believe that the so-called random events of life are anything less than God's appointed order. Be ready to discover His divine designs anywhere and everywhere.[10]

We don't need to know it all. We don't need to feel guilty for not paying better attention to the numerous advice columns in parenting magazines. Instead, we need to focus on what we *do* know. We know God will direct us by His Spirit as we acknowledge Him moment by moment throughout the day, seeing Him in every detail.

We know God will never leave us or forsake us. We know God loves our children and us completely. We know God has a good plan for our lives. Just check out Jeremiah 29:11!

On our parenting journey, we do many things for many reasons—guilt, fear, outside pressure, or because everyone else is doing it. But if we focused on God's guidance for us as we direct the ways of our children, how differently would our days be ordered? If we can focus on what we know about God, and His ways first—above the latest "good parent" advice—we'll have more peace about our decisions concerning our kids.

As Linda Ronstadt sang, "That may be all I need to know."

## Lead Me On

**A captive of the light, you say to me, lead me on....**

Teena Marie, *Top Gun* soundtrack, 1986, Sony Records

What message has God's Spirit spoken to you today about your children? What about yesterday, or the day before?

If you're like me, you're inspired after reading your Bible, or attending a worship service, or talking with Christian friends. But all too soon the old troubling worries and anxieties rear their ugly heads again.

I've experienced moments when I felt God's Spirit clearly speaking to me about my children. For example, one day I was working with my daughter on a story she was writing. As I sat there reading her words, I felt God saying, "You know, maybe I gave you *your* talents so you can foster *hers*."

Gary Thomas, the author of *Sacred Parenting,* had a time in his life when he also felt the Spirit of God speaking to him concerning one of his children. In fact, Gary felt that God was opening a specific door for his son Graham. He spoke to his wife about it, but never mentioned it to Graham.

Then one time, after coming back from retreat, Graham said, "You know, Mom, I really feel that God is calling me to do this."

Gary's wife smiled and answered, "You know, your father has known that for a couple of years."

"Why didn't he tell me?" Graham asked.

"Because he believes there are some things that you need to hear from God first."

The experience was a confirmation to their whole family.

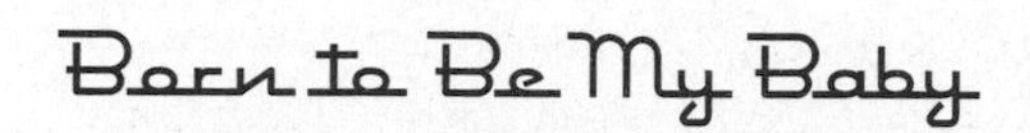


***Only God would know the reasons,***
***but I bet he must have had a plan....***

**Bon Jovi, *New Jersey*, 1988, Mercury**

Do you remember any moments in your parenting journey when God's Spirit spoke to you directly concerning your children? If so, take a few minutes to jot those times down. Make note of the impressions He placed upon your heart, or Scripture verses you felt were given just for them. If God leads you, share these things with your spouse or a friend.

Ask God to show you how to foster His desire in your children...not with your own willpower, but rather by allowing God's Spirit to work in you. Writing down these experiences will give you a written history of your "God advice." Your journal will also be a special treasure for your children, confirming God's path and plan in the years to come.

If God hasn't spoken to you in this way, ask Him to. Seek to know His heart about the purpose He's designed for each of your children.

## My Take On It

"I've felt like God's said different things about each of my girls. He's revealed areas of giftedness. He's also reminded me they're His more than ours. My wife and I, as their appointed guardians, are giving God free reign to work in them. God's message is that He wants them to know Him, so it's our responsibility to nurture them and to prepare them for when He draws near."

**—Bill, Illinois**
**Born in 1969, father of three**

"I have had the Holy Spirit bring a Scripture to mind for one of my children. It made me feel comforted…like I'm not on this journey alone."

**—Robin, Arkansas**
**Born in 1968, mother of three**

"I keep a journal for each child. It's hit or miss, but it is so encouraging to read back and see what God has already done in their young lives. I also know ultimately God entrusted these children to me because He knew I was the mom they would need. I take such comfort from that assurance on the days it's too much work or I feel completely incompetent."

**—Cara, Indiana**
**Born in 1974, mother of two**

"As a parent, I am engrained with a phrase said to me by my father as I was growing up: 'Would you rather be liked or respected?' It does not matter how many parenting books and self-help books I read; if I am not respected by my daughter, all the literature in the world will not help."

**—Jenna, Idaho**
**Born in 1976, mother of one**

## BONUS MATERIAL

Many of us may wonder why we need to be connected with the label "Gen X" at all. Isn't it better just to see ourselves as individuals instead of connecting with a whole group of people? The authors of *Mind the Gap* write:

> Tumultuous, life-changing events are impacting so strongly on a particular generation that it becomes branded or labeled for having lived in that era.[11]

So what were these tumultuous, life-changing events?

Dr. Rick and Kathy Hicks write in *Boomers, Xers, and Other Strangers: Understanding the Generational Differences That Divide Us:*

> The eighties were a rough time for kids to grow up. Their parents tended to be self-absorbed and distracted by things like making a living and finding their own fulfillment. There were many broken homes with single-parent families struggling to survive financially. A lot of kids were left to fend for themselves emotionally, if not physically. Latchkey kids (those who came home from school to an empty house) were common. Because of this, TV and movies (especially with the invention of the VCR) became an ever increasing source of values input. Older kids looked to peers, even gangs, for a sense of belonging or for role models that were missing in their homes.
>
> Political and environmental issues and events left these young people with the sense that the adults were ruining their futures, giving them a sense of hopelessness and cynicism. Moral failures of public figures, including parents, convinced them that people, especially older ones in established institutions, could probably not be trusted.

Many of the children of the eighties have an ingrained skepticism about life.[12]

Do you relate? I do. Yet, just because those things define our childhood era doesn't mean we have to dwell there. In fact, as you will see in the upcoming chapters, we Gen Xers are learning from our mistakes—working hard to give our kids what we most longed for.

# 4 Hard Habit to Break

## Shaking Past Habits

***I'm addicted to ya, babe....***

*Chicago, Chicago 17, 1984, Full Moon/Asylum*

Habits are hard to break. Very hard. Yet these are the very things I need to deal with in order to be the best parent I can be.

I don't know about you, but there are many "past issues" I had to deal with as a person before I was able to strive toward my potential as a mother. And since Gen Xers are all about being real... Well, let's just say it's confession time.

I first became a mom at age seventeen. My son was born three weeks after my high school graduation. There were about a million of us Gen Xer teens who had a baby that year. So, in a sense, we got a head start on this parenting thing.

While a teen pregnancy was hard to face, it was during my pregnancy I dedicated my life to Christ. My boyfriend was out of the picture. I'd dropped out of regular high school, and I had little hope. Then I remembered my Sunday school lessons about a Jesus who loved me, and I knew since I'd messed my life up so bad, it was worth giving Him a chance to fix it.

God worked amazingly after that. He brought a godly man into my life, and John and I were married when Cory was nine months old. Two more kids followed quickly after, and my husband and I set out to lead godly lives and build a godly family.

Looking back, one of the hardest things I've had to deal with was memories of my "past." And because this was deeply rooted in my heart, the regrets spilled over into every other aspect of my life...including my parenting.

I strove to do all the right things as I raised my kids. I loved them, read to them, prayed with them, told them about Jesus. I was encouraging and caring, yet I also disciplined them when needed. I chose to take my focus off my goals and dreams in order to homeschool them. Basically, I sacrificed what I wanted most for *me* in order to give my kids what I felt was best.

On the outside it seemed I was doing everything right, but on the inside I needed help. A lot of help.

You see, as the years passed, there were struggles which plagued me concerning my teen years. I had been intimate with guys. I'd had an abortion. I'd faced teen pregnancy...to name just a few.

Maybe you had other hang-ups during those years, but the effect is still the same—a heavy burden that weighs on your heart. Those memories are "there" no matter how you try to shake them.

Of course, there were other, smaller habits I also found hard to break, including a foul mouth, a snotty attitude, and longing for unhealthy media such as secular romance novels and soap operas.

Now don't get me wrong, I'm not going to make a list of things *I* think should be considered bad habits which you need to shake. I don't need to. You already feel convicted. You know those issues from the past that plague you, too.

Is there anything that God wants to speak to you about? If you're not sure, why don't you ask? Pause right now and ask God to point out any area where He's trying to get your attention and wants to work.

Here's a prayer I've prayed:

> Search me, O God, and know my heart; test me and know my anxious thoughts. See if there is any offensive way in me, and lead me in the way everlasting. (Psalm 139:23–24)

I've prayed this through the years, and sometimes I'm surprised by what God brings to mind. I've discovered *every time* I open my heart to God's perusal, there's always something He wants to work on, to clean up.

Saint Bernard of Clairvaux once wrote:

> You ask then how I knew [Jesus] was present, when His ways can in no way be traced? He is life and power, and as soon as He enters in, He awakens my slumbering soul; He stirs and soothes and pierces my heart, for before it was hard as stone, and diseased.[13]

Like good ol' Bernard, I can testify to the stirring and piercing. Breaking hard habits isn't easy, and sometimes they even require a jackhammer. Ouch.

Yet letting God work at digging out our bad habits is essential. Why? For starters, "Do what I say, not what I do" was one of my dad's favorite phrases during my growing up years…but we all know *that* doesn't happen! What we say, do, struggle with…is what our kids will say, do, struggle with. Whether we like it or not.

**You think you can instruct the ignorant and teach children the ways of God. For you are certain that in God's law you have complete knowledge and truth. Well then, if you teach others, why don't you teach yourself?**

(Romans 2:20–21, NLT)

## Somebody's Watching Me

***I always feel that somebody's watchin' me, is it just a dream?***

**ROCKWELL, SOMEBODY'S WATCHING ME, 1984, MOTOWN**

My daughter is thirteen, and I call her "mini me." When she answers the phone, people often think she's me. Leslie has the same tone as me, and her voice carries the same inflections. While she has her own collection of CDs, she rifles through my FFH, Newsboys, and Third Day because she likes that music, too. She's learned to put on makeup by watching me, and when she sees me engrossed in a good book, she naturally wants to read it. Leslie walks like me, talks like me, acts like me. She has some of my same convictions…and also some of my hang-ups.

When our kids are toddlers, we think it's so sweet when they pick up a block and place it to their ear like a cell phone. But the older they get, the more their mimicking matters…and if they aren't dealt with, the rock-solid bad habits in your life will most likely be theirs, too.

> In those days, when you were slaves of sin, you weren't concerned with doing what was right. And what was the result? It was not good, since now you are ashamed of the things you used to do, things that end in eternal doom. But now you are free from the power of sin and have become slaves of God. Now you do those things that lead to holiness and result in eternal life. (Romans 6:20–22, NLT)

What I love about this Scripture is the fact that Paul isn't trying to play down the past. Instead, he reminds fellow believers that what matters is what we are *now*: free from the power of sin and slaves of God.

The word *free* here means "to liberate,"[14] and this word has special meaning to me personally. A few years ago I wrote my first novel, *From Dust and Ashes.* It's about liberation from a Nazi concentration camp from the points of view of both an American GI who opened the camp gates and a prisoner inside. To write the book, I interviewed both veterans and survivors alike. I also attended a ceremony in Austria organized by the survivors to celebrate their *liberation* sixty years after the fact!

These men and women—prisoners of the Nazis—had been near death, oppressed, and hopeless. Yet their victors came, opened the gates, and offered them not only hope but a future, too. Once they walked from those gates, they were prisoners no more. They were liberated. They might revisit those times of bondage in their mind, but they no longer had to live behind the barbed wire. They did, however, have to realize their freedom and live in it, no longer behaving as if they were still in bondage.

Likewise, if we don't know the joy of true freedom in our hearts, how do we expect to lead our kids in this same freedom? Kids go where we take them; they have no choice. How sad it would be if our *own* inner struggles pulled our kids back to our past issues...merely because we ourselves had not yet fully realized our freedom in Christ.

> "If sin rules in me, God's life in me will be killed; if God rules in me, sin in me will be killed."
> **Oswald Chambers**[17]

## The Healing

It's taken me years to deal with some of the issues from my past. I've attended Bible studies for women who've had abortions. I helped start a crisis pregnancy center in our community. I've spoken at purity retreats for young women. And I mentor teenage mothers. For me, healing from my past involves helping others who face the same struggles. My heart is renewed when I help others find hope.

The additional benefit is that my children now have a mother who has wholeness in Christ. They've heard about my mistakes, and they've seen me reaching out. They've also gained conviction in these areas, following what I say...*and* what I do.

Being effective parents can only happen when we become whole in Christ. The following story from Max Lucado illustrates this beautifully:

> Here comes a young mother. With one hand she leads a child; with the other she drags her load, bumpy and heavy.
>
> Here comes an old man, face ravined with wrinkles. His trash sack is so long it hits the back of his legs as he walks. He glances at the woman and tries to smile.
>
> *What weight would he be carrying?* she wonders as he passes.
>
> "Regrets."
>
> She turns to see who spoke. Beside her on the bench sits a man. Tall, with angular cheeks and bright, kind eyes. Like hers, his jeans are mud stained. Unlike hers, his shoulders are straight. He wears a T-shirt and baseball cap. She looks around for his trash but doesn't see it.
>
> He watches the old man disappear as he explains. "As a young father, he worked many hours and neglected his family. His children don't love him. His sack is full, full of regrets."
>
> She doesn't respond. And when she doesn't, he does.
>
> "And yours?"
>
> "Mine?" she asks, looking at him.
>
> "Shame." His voice is gentle, compassionate.
>
> She still doesn't speak, but neither does she turn away.
>
> "Too many hours in the wrong arms. Last year. Last night... shame."[15]

Did you catch that? The woman led her child, yet was still carrying a burden that hindered them both. Think about your own life. What have you given up that's allowed you to follow Christ more easily and parent more effectively?

Now...what are you still holding onto?

It's worth hassling with, you know. The pain may be hard to face, but allowing God to mess with it and dig it out is worth it. Not only can you be an example in word and deed for your kids; there are a few other benefits, too. Max Lucado writes:

> When we surrender to God our cumbersome sacks, we don't just give up something; we gain something. God replaces them with a light-weight, tailor-made, sorrow-resistant attaché of gratitude.
>
> What will you gain with gratitude? You may gain your marriage. You may gain precious hours with your children. You may gain your self-respect. You may gain joy.[16]

## My Take On It

"It's very painful to think of the poor choices I made in the past—and the poor choices others made that affected me. But when I stop and think really hard about it, I begin to understand all the yucky stuff from the past is what makes me the compassionate, caring, loving person I am today."

**—Kristy, Texas**
**Born in 1971, mother of three**

"Sometimes it's easy to be a self-righteous parent. I think we Gen Xers are constantly comparing ourselves against other parents—and their own parents—to see how much better we are. We compare our sins, too, but often forget that pride is a big no-no in the Bible. Anger, pride, resentment, bitterness—these 'habits' or sins are no less devastating in the eyes of God, and they are probably more debilitating to our ability to parent well than, say, if I were a rehabilitated drug addict."

**—Heidi, Minnesota**
**Born in 1975, mother of two**

## My Take On It

"Yes, I believe that my shameful past has brought me to the Lord, made me into a kinder, less judgmental person. It has taught me to open my eyes and appreciate all the good things the Lord has given me in my life and thank Him on a daily basis for them. It has taught me not to take even the daily things for granted because it can all change in a heartbeat. I believe that because of this, my children know the Lord, they have had a better mother than I would have been before, and they witness a more loving relationship between my husband and myself. So it is true what the devil has planned for evil, the Lord changes to work for good."

**—Dee, Michigan**
**Born in 1975, mother of two**

"Jesus brings us freedom, but often it seems we don't believe it, or trust it, or act on it. I struggle with guilt. I know that Jesus forgives me. My problem is forgiving myself. Yet Psalm 32:5 says, 'Then I acknowledged my sin to you and did not cover up my iniquity. I said, "I will confess my transgressions to the LORD"—and you forgave the guilt of my sin.'

"That speaks freedom to me. God not only forgives my sin, but He forgives the guilt of my sin. This verse struck home and is helping me realize that God truly wants me to let it go, just as He has."

**—Lezlie, Minnesota**
**Born in 1967, mother of three**

"I was always the 'good kid,' so my issues aren't so much the shameful past, but being a perfectionist. The 'trash' I carry is taking on more than God wants me to. God says, 'My yoke is easy and my burden is light'—but I tend to give myself a heavy burden."

**—Michelle, New Jersey**
**Born in 1968, mother of one**

"I have a few things from the past I still carry with me that are very hard to let go of. I realize now I need to speak to God and have Him take this heavy luggage from me. He wants to give me freedom from whatever is burdening me. But being so independent for so long and not wanting help...it is very hard for me to do this."

**—Michelle W., New York**
**Born in 1973, mother of four**

## Don't You Forget About Me

***Tell me your troubles and doubts,***
***giving me everything inside and out....***

***SIMPLE MINDS, LIVE IN THE CITY OF LIGHT, 1985, VIRGIN RECORDS (USA)***

In the movie *Endless Sunshine of the Spotless Mind,* the characters played by Jim Carrey and Kate Winslet were heartbroken lovers who wished to wash the memories of their broken relationship from their minds. Through a type of fictionalized brain alteration, it worked...sort of. At the end of the movie, these two characters discover that even though their minds forgot, their hearts didn't...and they find themselves back together once again.

> Therefore...if you return, then I will restore you—before Me you will stand; and if you extract the precious from the worthless, you will become My spokesman. (Jeremiah 15:19, NASB)

In this verse, God is telling Jeremiah what He desires isn't that the prophet "forget" the worthless, but rather *extract* the precious from it. The word *precious* here is from the root word meaning "to be heavy" and "to make valuable."[18] It's taking those heavy things that are most important and becoming a spokesman for God concerning His truth.

Of course, these issues aren't always mistakes from the past. The burdens are as unique as each individual. For some it may be overachievement or a pessimistic attitude. Negative patterns we developed in our formative years can be just as heavy to bear as shameful regrets.

Just like us, our kids will mess up. Sometime, somehow. But what a great example we can model for them to mimic—transforming our past mistakes into future causes for Christ.

So what about you? What things weigh heavy on your heart? Ask God to help you extract them. And since you can't ignore them, study these issues in light of God's Word.

Now, what is God asking you to do with it? What type of example can you be for your kids? Think of the model you can be for God's restoration process—not only as you give it to God, but also as you struggle, turning to Christ and try again.

**Here's a word you can take to heart and depend on: Jesus Christ came into the world to save sinners. I'm proof—Public Sinner Number One—of someone who could never have made it apart from sheer mercy. And now he shows me off—evidence of his endless patience—to those who are right on the edge of trusting him forever.**

(1 Timothy 1:15–19
The Message)

# BONUS MATERIAL

## THE ATTITUDE OF EACH GENERATION TOWARD ITS PARENTS:

***GIs:*** My parents were Victorian and aloof.

***Silents:*** Hard-working and wise, but emotionally unavailable.

***Boomers:*** Too strict. I couldn't breathe; I had to rebel.

***Xers:*** Absent parents, worked too hard, and were too permissive.

***Millennials:*** They need all the help I can give them. Fairly harmless as parents.

## AND AS PARENTS THEMSELVES THEIR PARENTING STYLE:

***GIs:*** Victorian: aloof and cold.

***Silents:*** Authoritarian, dictatorial, controlling.

***Boomers:*** Permissive, detached, freeing, warm.

***Xers:*** Concerned, protective, deliberate.

***Millennials:*** We predict it will be relaxed and confident, and not smothering.[19]

# 5 Forever Young

## Striving for the Childhood I Never Had

***Can you imagine when this race is won, turn our golden faces into the sun....***

ALPHAVILLE, *FOREVER YOUNG*, 1984, ATLANTIC (USA)

I can't tell you how many times I fell for the deception that real life starts tomorrow.

"After this book deadline..."

"Once I finish this project..."

"After the holidays..."

"When I get organized..."

"...*then* I'll have time to do this parenting thing right!"

The untruth of this notion hit me one day while I grappled with a pile of overdue library books and dirty laundry stacked at the top of the stairs. As I bolted for the bathroom to throw my hair up in a ponytail and slip into sweatpants, my mind raced with the two dozen things I needed to accomplish that day: homework to grade, bathrooms to clean, phone calls to return, children to drive around, deadlines to meet.

I chided myself yet again, *Tomorrow I'll wake up earlier. I'll get my act together. I'll check homework papers and pull something from the freezer to defrost in the morning instead of making spaghetti for the third time this week. I'll take ten minutes and introduce myself to the new neighbor. I'll make that eye appointment...*

*Tomorrow.*

Mixed in with my thoughts were the sounds of two children arguing and a third pleading with me to hurry before she was late for her piano lesson. The dog barked at the UPS truck rumbling by, and the phone rang.

Then it hit me. As I stood there, hairbrush in one hand and toothbrush in the other, I realized, *This is life.*

Life isn't what will happen tomorrow or next week, when everything "settles down." Life is now. Today. This moment.

I read, "This is the day that the LORD has made; let us rejoice and be glad in it" (Psalm 118:24, ESV). Yet instead of lifting my heart, the impact of those words sometimes hits me in the gut like a fist.

How often do I rejoice in my busy, crazy, jumbled days? Almost never. Instead, I rejoice—and find hope—in the idea of a tomorrow where everything works as it should and real life can begin.

"This is life," I repeated to my image in the mirror. "This is what my kids will remember. When they look back twenty years from now and think about their childhood, they will remember days like today."

Some of the Gen Xers out there may recall these words sung by Alphaville: "Sooner or later they all will be gone...I want to be forever young."

Yet my kids—*our* kids—won't be forever young. And even as I hope that *tomorrow* I'll get it right, I have to face that they're growing up *today.*

*Standing firm means living the life God has handed you, without explanation, without apology.*

—Donna Partow[20]

## My Take On It

"I love to share my childhood with my children. I love to tell stories and relate memories. We take our kids camping and to Disney World, because those are the childhood memories that I love. The books I enjoyed as a child I read again, and somehow it is like discovering them for the first time. Thanks to eBay, I can get my children the same toys I loved. Plus, I have a second chance to play with Strawberry Shortcake. How great is that?"

**—Jennifer R., Wisconsin**
**Born in 1969, mother of three**

"My biggest regrets were not taking chances. If I had my teenage years to do again, I would live life to its fullest, be as involved as I can be—take up an instrument, try out for the cheerleading team, not back out on my best friends in a talent show dance. How does that affect me as a parent? I want to give my children every opportunity to have a variety of experiences so they will not have the same regrets."

**—Beth, Washington**
**Born in 1970, mother of four**

## Today Matters

I realize that today matters. But that doesn't mean I don't strive for this image of perfection cocooned and protected in my mind. There's always a hope that I'll finally experience the day when the house is clean *and* organized, the bills are paid, and the kids entertain themselves. Yet, frankly, I also realize even if the miracle ever happened, it would last for all of point two seconds.

If you're like me, you may feel the ideal life, the perfect family, is out there—somewhere beyond your grasp. That getting your priorities straight, attending the right parenting classes, being a good role model, and choosing the right playmates for your kids will get you "there."

Author John Fischer calls this the Big Christian Lie: "It's the belief that someone, somewhere, is getting it right."[21]

And while we may realize with our rationale that no one will have a perfect household, the perfect life, something within still longs for this very thing.

"He has made everything beautiful in its time" (Ecclesiastes 3:11). Surely that means someday my kids, my life, my house will eventually get "there," right?

I used to hope that way...until I read the rest of the verse. "He has also set eternity in the hearts of men; yet they cannot fathom what God has done from beginning to end" (v. 11).

God has put something in us that *longs for* perfection. He gave us this longing to ultimately pull us to Him, the only true perfect being. Yet we keep looking for it on earth and feel it is always "just out of our grasp." This not only relates to our home, jobs, and physical bodies, but also to our children—or more to the point, to their *childhoods*.

A few of you reading this book (I'm sure there are one or two of you out there) grew up in childhood homes where a wonderful, godly example was modeled. But most of us sense in our hearts that we missed out. Our childhood doesn't match up to the ideal we fantasized about. And because of our longings, our unmet desires from our childhood, those things we wanted most as children are now the *very things* we work hardest to provide for our kids.

I have a perfect example.

Growing up, I lived in a family of nonreaders. While my mom was wonderful in many ways, I can't remember a single time when she sat down and read to me. Not one picture book. Not one chapter book. Nothing. It wasn't until the fifth grade that I discovered a love for reading. My family had moved into a rental house less than two miles from the library. With nothing else to do, I visited after school and on weekends. I even volunteered there during the summer. (In those days, a fifth grader was allowed to ride her bike two miles alone without anyone thinking a thing about it.)

When I had my kids, I knew one thing for sure: We would be a family of readers. Even before my babies comprehended the words, I placed them on my lap with a pile of books at my side. As they grew older, I continued to buy book after book—so many that today they don't all fit on our massive bookshelves. And that's not even factoring in our frequent trips to the library. The librarians at our local branch know our names and phone number by heart. They even have a special shelf under the front counter labeled "Goyers." (You probably think I'm making that up!)

I'd like to say that my going overboard with books is my *only* example of overcompensation, but that's far from the case. Looking back, I see there are many things I always wanted as a child, but never had, got, or did. So guess what Cory, Leslie, and Nathan have, get, and do!

The problem isn't my desire to give my kids the best; it's that I'm attempting to fulfill the longings of my childhood, my "forever young," by living vicariously through my children's youth. *Ouch.*

*Someone, somewhere, is getting it right,* I tell myself. And "right" in my mind is everything I missed out on and longed for. These longings influence my decisions more than anything else.

## Longings

So what are the longings of Generation X parents?

One is to be more present in our children's everyday lives. Graeme Codrington and Sue Grant-Marshall write in *Mind the Gap:*

> The boomers' permissive style of parenting left their children, the Xers, so much to their own devices that Xers are labeled the lonely,

> latchkey generation, who let themselves into empty homes after school. Now Xers in their turn are making extraordinary efforts to create a balance between work and home so that they can be with their families.[22]
>
> Another longing of Gen X parents is to have a better quality of life.
>
> Generation X members are entering the parenting arena in increasing numbers. These young parents, ranging in age from twenty-five to forty, are more concerned about their overall quality of life than playing super-parent.[23]

Other issues we deal with include wanting to give our kids more than we had (we grew up in a recession, remember?); wanting them to participate in the extracurricular activities for which our parents didn't have the time, money, or interest; wanting to protect them from "growing up too quickly"; and wanting to give them the right education, the right morals, and the right attitudes to succeed in life.

These longings aren't bad, of course, when we line them up with our holy God, and realize that *our* plans matter little in comparison to *His.*

> God-of-the-Angel-Armies speaks: "Exactly as I planned, it will happen. Following my blueprints, it will take shape." (Isaiah 14:24, *The Message*)

The word *planned* here is translated "compare."[24] It's as if God has weighed the different possibilities, looked at them from all angles, and then chose the best way. He makes the blueprints...then He constructs them into our reality.

And our kids' reality. *This* is the childhood the Lord has for our kids. Not the childhood *we* wished we'd had, or the perfect life we can never attain, but the blueprints and the form *He* is fashioning into reality.

"Remember your history, your long and rich history. I am God, the only God you've had or ever will have—incomparable, irreplaceable—from the very beginning telling you what the ending will be, all along letting you in on what is going to happen, assuring you, 'I'm in this for the long haul, I'll do exactly what I set out to do.'" (Isaiah 46:10–11, *The Message*)

It's okay to remember your longings as a child. It's okay to dream up what you wish you could give your kids. In future chapters, we'll talk more about how to consider our kids and their gifts, and *then* make choices concerning what activities we sign them up for, and what expectations we have of them. But even before we worry about that, the first step is not to let *your* desires motivate you; instead, let *His*.

God has longings for your children even greater than lost childhood. He's willing to tell us these things as we seek Him out.

## My Take On It

"I wonder if there is such a thing as normal. If so, what does it look like? Unfortunately, I think we strive for the ideal 'normal' when it's different for everyone, and in trying to achieve that Norman Rockwell setting, we forget the most important times, those teaching moments that God gives us amongst the chaos we call life."

**—Jenny W., Texas**
**Born in 1970, mother of four**

> "God's reminding me that the blueprint He has for our kids is the perfect one for them and the times they are growing up in. He's forming them in the image He needs for the works He plans in their lives. Without the foundations He's laying now, through us (and at times despite us) our kids would not be prepared to do all He will require of them later in life. This isn't a license to give up on parenting. It is instead the holy job we have been called to, and it requires us to stay in step with the Holy Spirit for our daily marching orders."
>
> **—Allison, Florida**
> **Born in 1974, mother of two**

## Good Plans

It's easy to realize God has good plans. It's much harder to figure out what they are and apply them to your family.

> But the plans of the LORD stand firm forever, the purposes of his heart through all generations. (Psalm 33:11)

So how do you determine God's plans for your family and your kids? Here are four biggies to start with:

1. **Think big.** Discovering our plans for our family begins by determining God's plans for generations. Sit down with your Bible and consider His plans for all of us—salvation, living holy lives, interacting with a body of believers, sharing the good news of Jesus. Then ask, "Is my family in line with these plans?" If not, ask God for the first step in making His plans for generations a reality in your home. After that first step is in motion (with the wisdom and strength that comes from God alone), ask for the next one.

2. **Think high.**

> "My thoughts are completely different from yours," says the LORD. "And my ways are far beyond anything you could imagine. For just as the heavens are higher than the earth, so are my ways higher than your ways and my thoughts higher than your thoughts." (Isaiah 55:8–9, NLT)

Prayerfully ask God to reveal His thoughts, and then open His Word as He speaks them. If your children are old enough, visualize searching out the will of God through the Word as a voyage of discovery you're embarking on together.

3. **Think in.** E. M. Bounds writes in *Power Through Prayer*:

> God's plan is to make much of the man, far more of him than of anything else. Men are God's method. The Church is looking for better methods; God is looking for better men.[25]

I think the same can be said of families. How can you help your family members become better men, women, boys, and girls of God? Methods come and go, but who we are in Christ is transferable to eternity.

I've heard it said that God is more interested in the process than the product. It's the process that will draw us into a deeper, more abiding relationship with Him. The product of our obedience is a bonus.

4. **Think prepared.** Oswald Chambers tells us:

> Readiness for God means that we are prepared to do the smallest thing or the largest thing—it makes no difference. Whenever any duty presents itself, we hear God's voice as our Lord heard His Father's voice.... Jesus Christ expects to do with us

> just as His Father did with Him. He can put us wherever He wants, in pleasant duties or in menial ones, because our union with Him is the same as His union with the Father.[26]

Where is God opening doors in our lives? What messages is He placing on our hearts? These are not random occurrences, but areas where He desires to work.

In fact, this fourth point will be a natural result when we strive for points one, two, and three. Once we realize God's plans for generations, discover His thoughts through His Word, and strive to be obedient children of God, *then* our hearts will be prepared for His plans and our ears will be open to His voice.

This encourages me to know that even days which seem far from "perfection" (yes, those days) are the exact ones God has considered, chosen, and shaped for my family…for this time in history…dirty laundry and overdue library books included.

## My Take On It

"I'm not sure if my kids would yet understand the idea of 'going on an adventure to find God's will in our family's life' entirely, but I know that they can understand in small pieces.

"For example, recently my son mentioned not really liking someone at school. At the time I didn't think much about it, but several days later I was invited to a party that I knew would be attended by someone with whom I just don't 'click.' I found it the perfect opportunity to ask my son what I should do. He told me what God would want me to do, which helped him, too. Later he asked how the party went and how I acted. I was glad to be able to say I had done what God reminded us both to do."

**—Shannon, Colorado**
**Born in 1971, mother of two**

"I have been a mother for seven years, and I'm realizing that what I see in magazines and television is not reality. I need to stop reaching for this unattainable status of 'perfect life/having it all together' and focus on my family, because God chose me to be the mother of my children for who I am, not what my status is."

**—Andrena, Michigan**
**Born in 1974, mother of three**

# BONUS MATERIAL

## WHY GENERATION X?

American sociologists decided that babies born from 1983 onwards would be called Millennials, as they would end their schooling in the new century. As generations are born roughly twenty years apart, that means the Xers were given 1963 for their birth date because it is a halfway date between 1942 and 1983 and is nothing significant for anything much more than that.... Xers are defined more for what they are *not* than by what they are. They are caught between other important dates in American history—and not defined by being born at a significant time.[27]

*"I believe a cloud has hung over the head of our generation, but that's what makes God so amazing. He wants us to rise above labels and become the generation He created us to be."*

*—Cara, Indiana*
*Born in 1974, mother of two*

# 6 I'LL Stand BY YOU

## Parenting Roles Through the Ages and Stages

***Don't be ashamed to cry, let me see you through....***

*THE PRETENDERS, LAST OF THE INDEPENDENTS, 1994, SIRE RECORDS (USA)*

There was a time when I thought my kids would never be out of diapers. When I couldn't imagine taking a shower without a tiny fist pounding on the bathroom door. When I only dreamed of watching an entire movie without a small head peeking into the living room, asking for a "dwink" of water for the tenth time.

I used to inwardly groan when older ladies approached in the grocery store and advised cheerfully, "Enjoy them while they are young, dear. They grow so quickly." Now I find I'm the one giving that advice to other young moms I meet.

The problem with parenting is...once you get one stage figured out, your kids are on to something new.

This is a good thing for our kids—they need to grow, and learn, and change. I suppose, it's good for us, too. Since each age and stage brings its own set of unique challenges, we find it absolutely necessary to seek God's help. As they grow and learn, so do we.

Gen X mom Jenn Doucette, author of *The Velveteen Mommy*, makes this observation:

> Can you recall what you were like before you had children? Unencumbered? Unfettered? Uninterrupted? Thinner? I can relate to the Velveteen Rabbit with sateen-lined ears. Perched upon my hospital bed the day our son was born, painkillers racing through my system, I felt quite splendid and charming. But the freshness of motherhood rubbed off, much like the newness of the Velveteen Rabbit.
>
> In an astonishing twist of Providence, God uses the true pain of motherhood to shape us, mold us, grow us, transform us, and make us Real—more like Himself: "Therefore we do not lose heart. Though outwardly we are wasting away, yet inwardly we are being renewed day by day" (2 Corinthians 4:16).[28]

Just like the Velveteen Rabbit, reaching "Real" as a parent takes time. Thankfully, God gives us eighteen years—and everything from teething to drivers' education classes—to work on it.

## My Take On It

"I'm trying to hide in my basement to escape the fact that moms don't truly get a vacation. I'd like to be happy about that…but today I'm just exhausted. This reminder helps me refocus on the truth: The stresses and pains of this life are momentary. Not only that, but they are actually what God uses to make me more like Him—real. I love that!"

**—Amy, Georgia**
**Born in 1971, mother of three**

"Sometimes I forget that the hard times as a mom help me grow as a Christian. I can rely on God even in daily stuff with my kids, and I know that He's smiling at me when I keep trying, even though it's rough."

**—Katie, Montana**
**Born in 1972, mother of two**

"Some of the biggest challenges I face aren't with society, they're right in my home. How do I know which battles to pick? Is it okay that I just burst into tears in front of the kids? Of all the mistakes I make, are any of them going to send my kids into years of therapy?

"Some days all I can do is stop, pray, and hope that what comes out of my mouth next is straight from God. When I'm open to His hand dictating my day, there's such a calm presence in the flow."

**—Mona, Arizona**
**Born in 1974, mother of three**

## I'll Be Loving You (Forever)

***We've come too far, to ever turn back now....***

***New Kids on the Block, Hangin' Tough, 1988, Columbia (USA)***

To make things simple, I've narrowed the stages of parenthood down to the three biggies:

1. The "Do What I Say" stage
2. The "This Is *Why* You Do What I Say" stage
3. The "Follow Me as I Do" stage

Believe it or not, the first stage is the easiest. After all, you know what is right and wrong; your child doesn't. You tell your child what he/she needs to do and your child obeys. (At least, that's how it's *supposed* to work.) In the earliest years, there shouldn't be long dialogues of explanation. Your goal—and their job—is obedience.

The second stage includes more work. Children still need to obey, but it's the parents' job to tell them the *reason behind the request*. Why do we throw our chewing gum in the trash instead of on the sidewalk? Because there are others who are coming behind us...and we need to think about them.

The goal is still obedience...but instead of robot-like responses, our children must come to a place where they learn to think of others beyond themselves. It is during this stage that kids discover they are not the center of the universe. (Never mind the fact that you probably know an adult or two who has missed this stage completely!)

The final stage is the most challenging for the mere fact that we must model more than lecture. In other words, we need to live out the lives we desire our children to imitate.

Now that my children are preteens and teens, most of the training that takes place involves being an example of godly living. Yes, I still make requests of my children. And, yes, they still obey...but that encompasses—at most—only 5 percent of our day. The rest of the time is spent showing them what a Christian looks like at the grocery store, with neighbors, in the church body, and through volunteering efforts, and then talking to them about how God's truth applies in each of those situations.

At this stage, my husband and I don't sit down and write out a ten-step plan on what lessons we desire to teach our children. Instead, we let God guide our lives. We are models of seeking, prayer, Bible study, praise, and service. With our words, actions, and lives, we show how being a Christian works.

Of course, since nobody's perfect (especially me!) this modeling also includes confessions after we mess up, repentance, and asking the Holy Spirit to fill us so we can do better next time.

Tedd Tripp writes in *Shepherding a Child's Heart*:

> The parent is the child's guide. As the shepherd, you want to help your child understand himself as a creature made by and for God. You cannot show him these things merely by instruction; you must lead him on a path of discovery. You must shepherd his thoughts, helping him to learn discernment and wisdom.
>
> This shepherding process is a richer interaction than telling your child what to do and think. It involves investing your life in your child with open and honest communication that unfolds the meaning and purpose of life. It is not simply direction, but direction in which there is self-disclosure and sharing. Values and spiritual vitality are not simply taught, but caught.[29]

I don't know about you, but *that* is the type of parent I want to be. It is also the type of parent I wish I'd had. As much as I respect and love my parents, that wasn't the type of role models I grew up with. Maybe you feel the same.

In *Mind the Gap*, Codrington and Grant-Marshall observe:

> Boomer children are famous, or notorious, for being raised on what has been described as Dr. Benjamin Spock's "permissiveness." But the impact of Dr. Spock's influence was felt fully when boomers themselves *became parents* and thoroughly embraced his less restrictive attitude.
>
> [Gen Xers] grew up in an "anti-child" era as their Boomer (and a few Silent) generation parents focused more on their own personal needs. They quoted Dr. Benjamin Spock, saying that the best gift you could give your children was a happy parent. To achieve this status, you had to focus on doing your own thing. Boomers, remembering the stifling control that was imposed on them by their own Silent/GI parents, went to the opposite extreme, and allowed young Xers inordinate freedom.[30]

"Youth with inordinate freedom" is one way to put it. "Youth out of control" is another. (Don't you wonder why they named us Generation X? Some claim it is because we were completely "crossed out"—dismissed as a generation that would never come to any good.)

So where does that leave us as a generation of parents? For one thing, it helps us understand that this parenting thing isn't something we can accomplish without making some mistakes. Even parents with the best intentions mess up.

It also proves God can take our challenges as kids and redeem them, giving us new convictions with our own children. Whether we were raised in the model home or not, each of us should realize as our ultimate goal the same goal Paul had—to labor "until Christ is formed in [them]" (Galatians 4:19).

> We proclaim him, admonishing and teaching everyone with all wisdom, so that we may present everyone perfect in Christ. To this end I labor, struggling with all his energy, which so powerfully works in me. (Colossians 1:28–29)

And you thought labor ended when that baby popped out!

Of course, it's easy to get stressed out if we focus only on verse 28. "Present everyone perfect in Christ"? What a huge task!

That's why it's so important to continue on to read (and reread) verse 29: "Struggling with all his energy, which *so powerfully works* in me."

Do you notice it's *His* power that works powerfully? It's not about what I can offer as a parent, but rather what I allow Christ to do through me. He is the powerful one. The wise one. The complete one without hang-ups or holdbacks. To get a clearer picture of this, read Paul's explanation in Romans 11:34–36:

> Everything comes from him;
> Everything happens through him;
> Everything ends up in him.
> Always glory! Always praise! (*The Message*)

Don't you love that? Everything comes from Him. And everything means *everything*...including the mighty power to succeed at this parenting thing.

But how do we tap into that power?

> Be strong in the Lord and in the strength of His might. (Ephesians 6:10, NASB)

Wesley L. Duewel writes in *Let God Guide You Daily*:

> Your Counselor indwells in you all the time. He is resident to guide you in all your activities. Since that is His special role to you. He desires to interweave His guidance with all parts of your living.[31]

Isn't that what we need most in the ages and stages of *parenthood*—His guidance, interwoven with all parts of our living? The best thing about depending on His power to "work mightily in me" is that the benefit is two-fold. When Christ's power is working to help us shepherd our children, it's also molding *us* in the process.

Blaise Pascal wrote, "Not only do we not know God except through Jesus Christ; we do not even know ourselves except through Jesus Christ."[32]

So while our goal may be focused on the ages and stages of our children, God's goal also concerns the ages and stages of *their* parents.

> Then *we* will no longer be *like children*, forever changing our minds about what we believe because someone has told us something different or because someone has cleverly lied to us and made the lie sound like the truth. Instead, *we* will hold to the truth in love, becoming more and more in every way like Christ. (Ephesians 4:14–15, NLT)

So who is training whom? The way it should work is that God trains us *as* we train our kids. That way we all may become complete in Christ.

The Shepherd leading the shepherding parents. Now *that* is very cool.

## My Take On It

"As an attorney, I love teaching the reason behind the request. I'm essentially teaching my five-year-old logic. 'Why can't I do that?' she asks. I respond, 'Because if you do, this is the result, and it's a bad result. This is for your protection.'"

**—Cara, Indiana**
**Born in 1974, mother of two**

"A verse that has given me great comfort is Isaiah 40:11: 'He tends his flock like a shepherd: He gathers the lambs in his arms and carries them close to his heart; he gently leads those that have young.'

"That's me! He's leading me! Thank you, God for leading me. I am not alone!"

**—Lezlie, Minnesota**
**Born in 1967, mother of three**

"I grew up going to church and hearing different Bible stories. Although my parents encouraged me in knowing about Jesus, I found out about a personal relationship with him outside of our home. In contrast, I want our children to remember their dad and me walking daily with Jesus…that's our desire for them. We present Jesus as a normal part of life, not just someone you hear about on occasion or just at church."

**—Jenn, New York**
**Born in 1972, mother of one**

"There is a time and place for direct obedience without comprehension, but it's more meaningful when we understand why we do what we do. Just like in my walk with the Lord, I want to obey Him because I love Him and want to please Him—and not just because He said so, or because I'm afraid I'll get zapped if I don't follow His commandments."

**—Michelle, Arizona**
**Born in 1967, mother of two**

# BONUS MATERIAL

## BABIES ARE "IT"

The arrival of the first Millennial babes in the 1980s marked a dramatic societal shift from the latchkey kids. If the key on the string around their necks symbolized the Xers, then the "Baby on Board" car stickers mark a new era in which babies were not only seen and heard but actually became status symbols.

Suddenly, pregnancy and infants are hot stuff. Take a look at the glossy, celebrity-obsessed magazines.... Xers flaunt their pregnancies, wandering around shopping malls exposing their huge, bare bellies with pride to the world.

Millennials arrived already adored, desired, demanded and cosseted before they uttered their first cry. They've had music played to them in the womb, stories read to them, powerful and positive thoughts relayed to them. In fact, the new status symbol is a stay-at-home mom.

As Xers began having babies, so they reacted against their lonely, unprotected upbringing. They do so in a completely natural, instinctive manner, unlike the Boomers who set out to discover 'family values' as a conscious and deliberate lifestyle choice. *Time* magazine ran a feature in which they described the Generation Xer as "Gen Nester"... as these adored darlings have grown from toddlers into teens, their every step and utterance (not forgetting the actual birth) have been recorded on video and digital camera and instantly downloaded by their worldwide families and friends. The world has changed to accommodate them.[33]

# 7 Words into Action

## Minding Thoughts, Taming Tongues

***I will hold you to the promises you've made....***

JERMAINE JACKSON, *PRECIOUS MOMENTS*, 1986, ARISTA

Graeme Codrington writes in *Generation X Papers: 25 Sentences That Define a Generation*:

> Xers don't ask "Is it true?" but rather "Does it work?" Something may be true, and even accepted by them as such, but they don't care unless it really affects their lives. They want real answers to their real-life issues.[34]

So what is real-life to Gen Xers? What our minds tell us, of course.

Maybe we're just stubborn. We can hear something a thousand times, but until *we* believe it—truly believe it—it doesn't make one iota of difference.

In point of fact, here's how it works with me: I live in Montana. Outside, the sky is gray and a layer of snow covers the ground. My house is a white, two-story at the end of the road.

In the northeast corner is my office. It's here I type these words. Praise music is flowing from my CD player, and I'm sipping from a mug of room-temperature coffee because I'm too lazy to get up and pour myself a fresh cup.

If you were to ring my doorbell, like my neighbor did a few minutes ago, what I've just described is what you would see. Yet there's another world within this one that you would not have access to unless I clued you in.

Carried around within my gray matter, regardless of my external circumstances or surroundings, is what I affectionately like to think of as The Land of Tricia's Thoughts. It's here I dream up grand visions and lament things I wouldn't confess within the pages of a book. It's in this private oasis that I evaluate and scrutinize. This inner space is as real to me in a crowd as when I'm completely alone.

The thousands of me-to-me conversations going on throughout the day are labeled by psychologists as "self-talk." The more I parent, the more I realize how much this inner self-talk affects my outer world.

I recently read this quote from John Lembo: "Every waking moment we talk to ourselves about the things we experience. Our self-talk, the thoughts we communicate to ourselves, in turn control the way we feel and act." It reminded me of a quote on a small plaque that used to hang in my kitchen: "If mama ain't happy, ain't nobody happy." How true that statement is! My thoughts affect my attitude and my words. My attitude and my words determine the mood in our home.

There are times when I don't come right out and tell my kids I'm sick and tired of picking up after them, but my furrowed brow and deep sigh give my true feelings away. (Okay, the hand on the hip may be a good indicator, too.)

I would like to say I don't have major problems with negative self-talk anymore, but it's just not true. Only a few days ago I was struggling with an issue that I couldn't shake—in fact, it was one of the worst struggles of my life. I kept talking about this battle to anyone who would listen, mostly my husband and friends. And even when no one was around to hear my complaints, my inner world replayed them like a needle stuck on a record.

Finally, my husband had had enough. He (lovingly) urged me, "Say, 'I have a wonderful life.' Say, 'God loves me completely and my husband cherishes me.' Say 'God has blessed me, continues to bless me, and I am thankful.' Tell yourself those things until your heart believes them."

I began repeating these words. It was hard at first. I wanted to pout, not rejoice. But as I continued repeating these phrases, the discontent emotions faded, and thankfulness filled my inner world.

"He who would be useful, strong, and happy must cease to be a passive receptacle for the negative, beggarly, and impure streams of thought," James Allen once wrote. "And as a wise householder commands his servants and invites his guests, so must he learn to command his desires and to say, with authority, what thoughts he shall admit into the mansion of his soul."

Relentless, repetitive self-talk transforms our self-image—for the good or for the bad. It modifies both our inner and outer worlds.

"I will hold you to the promises you made," Jermaine Jackson sang. And that's the same thing our emotions, our will, and body language say: "We will do, oh thoughts, what you tell us to."

## My Take On It

"Ever since my parents were divorced (when I was fourteen), I have struggled with problems with my thought life. I would create new worlds in my mind to explore, anything different that would take me away from the reality of my life that I despised. Even now as an adult I find myself 'slipping away' in my thoughts when I don't like what's going on around me. It drains me mentally and emotionally of precious energy—energy I need to keep on track as a mother."

**—Judy, New York**
**Born in 1965, mother of two**

"Whatever the situation, my son believes the outcome will be the worst-case scenario. He's a 'glass half empty' person. This confuses me, since I tend to always see the best in people and the best in any situation. I need to help him with his self-talk. I need to try to teach him how to speak to himself in positive, truthful ways."

—Lisa P., Nevada
Born in 1969, mother of three

## Can't Fight This Feeling

***You give my life direction, you make everything so clear....***

**REO SPEEDWAGON, WHEELS ARE TURNIN', 1985, EPIC (USA)**

Surely you desire truth in the inner parts; you teach me wisdom in the inmost place. (Psalm 51:6)

The words *inner parts* here are figuratively translated "inmost thoughts."[35] But more than that, these words relate a sense of "overlaying" or being "covered." The truth spoken of in this verse isn't just something plopped or dropped in, but rather something wrapped around, secured, as a complete covering.

God desires His truth to cover all our thoughts. Isn't that an awesome concept?

Even more than that, the word *truth* here is translated "stability." Something that is "built up and supported, assured, and established as faithful."[36]

I don't know about you, but there's a distinction between the thoughts I invite into my inner world and those God establishes. My thoughts are anything but stable. They waver and change. They accuse when they should praise. They mock when they should trust.

That's why it's so important for me not to trust my thoughts...but instead seek God's. And that's exactly what He wants for us, too.

If you need wisdom—if you want to know what God wants you to do—ask him, and he will gladly tell you. He will not resent you asking. But when you ask him, be sure that you really expect him to answer, for a doubtful mind is as unsettled as a wave of the sea that is driven and tossed by the wind. People like that should not expect to receive anything from the Lord. They can't make up their minds. They waver back and forth in everything they do." (James 1:5–8, NLT)

*Ouch.* That hit too close to my "innermost parts" for comfort. So what's a parent to do? We know our lives, our families, and the training up of our kids can be *transformed* if we depend upon God's thoughts above our own…but where do we start?

1. Confess. Robert Benson writes in *Living Prayer*:

> We cannot be filled with God until we are not so full of ourselves. Our hearts and minds, wonderful as they are, are simply too small. We cannot give our hearts to God, or anyone else for that matter, as long as they are too heavy for us to lift.[37]

Benson goes on to say:

> In any interior life, there are times when we do not know how to proceed, when we are uncertain as to the choices we are to make, when we cannot choose between this thing or that. We need a word, the Word for us.
>
> You cannot hear the Word right now…because there is no room in you for the Word right now. You must live in confession for a while, until you are empty enough to receive the Word.[38]

There are a lot of things we can fill our minds with, but confession is the one thing that empties it. It's hard admitting our failures, our limitations, and our fears. We don't like to think about the pain we've inflicted on others, the thoughts that found their way in, or the words that made their way out. But it's here, at this place of humility, where we clean out in order to "hear." Only then can diving into God's Word and singing God's praises stick.

As I was going through my recent struggle, I realized that to deal with my thoughts I needed to confess them. I talked to my husband first and close friends later. And it was only when I laid myself bare that I found release from what was plaguing me. Finally, joy replaced discontent.

2. **Talk truth.** Some wise person has labeled our repeated thoughts "self-fulfilling prophecies." In other words, if we keep talking about something long enough, it's sure to happen. Thus, talking about our goals and desires will move us in that direction. Replaying in our mind our weaknesses and struggles—things we can't overcome—will accomplish the same thing.

I've had to work on this not only in my own life, but also in my kids' lives: "I'm not good at math." "I can't learn that instrument." "This is too hard." Hearing these words tell me two things:

1. My kids need help with *their* inner world and thoughts.

2. What they speak is what they will fulfill.

So it's my job to make sure they're speaking truth according to God's Word.

I also encourage my children to "talk up" what they'd like to see happen in their lives. For example, my sixteen-year-old son talks about *when*, not *if*, his first novel will be published. To hear him speak about his dream shows me that he's set this desire in his heart. It also helps those around him to keep him accountable.

3. **Become Spirit dependent.** In John 14:16–17, Jesus said, "I will ask the Father, and he will give you another Counselor to be with you forever—the Spirit of truth. The world cannot accept him, because it neither sees him nor knows him. But you know him, for he lives with you and will be in you." In addition to the truth we have in the Word of God, we also have the Spirit of Truth within us.

   The Christian musical group Casting Crowns speaks about this in one of their songs: "The voice of Truth tells me a different story," they sing. "The voice of Truth says, 'Do not be afraid.'" And, like the song says, out of all the voices out there...the voice of Truth, which is the voice of the Holy Spirit, is the one I choose to listen to and believe.

4. **Trust in the Word of God.** Kenneth Copley writes in *The Great Deceiver*:

> The solution to any lie is the supernatural illumination that comes from the Holy Spirit and the holy Word of God. Only truth can dispel a lie.
>
> Through the Spirit of God, Jesus takes what is in the Word of God and makes it practical and effective in our lives. He answers our questions, shows us how to deal with difficult situations, and guides us through the "valley of the shadow of death" when necessary.[39]

Any time we face negative thoughts, the final authority we need to turn to is the Word of God.

Do your thoughts tell you truth is relative? Jesus said, "I am the way and the truth and the life. No one comes to the Father except through me" (John 14:6).

Do your thoughts tell you God doesn't care about your parenting struggles?

"There is a friend who sticks closer than a brother" (Proverbs 18:24).

Do your thoughts tell you that being part of a church body isn't an important part of being a Christian? "The church of the living God [is] the pillar and foundation of the truth" (1 Timothy 3:15).

Check out this passage from Hebrews 10:23–25:

> **Let us hold fast the confession of our hope without wavering, for He who promised is faithful; and let us consider how to stimulate one another to love and good deeds, not forsaking our own assembling together, as is the habit of some, but encouraging one another; and all the more as you see the day drawing near. (NASB)**

What does the Truth do in our lives? "For in [God] you have been enriched in every way—in all your speaking and in all your knowledge" (1 Corinthians 1:5).

Ask God to enrich your words and thoughts. Confess, talk truth, and depend on the Spirit within you. Use God's Word to combat any lie that attempts to fill your mind. Doing this will transform your inner world and spill into your outer one.

Test this concept on yourself, and try it on your kids. In moments of joy and moments of struggle, ask your children what's going on in their thought lives. Then help *them* distinguish the voice of Truth from the lies.

REO Speedwagon may sing, "I've been running around in circles in my mind," but thankfully we can stand firm in the steadfastness of God's truth. Why don't you try it today?

## My Take On It

"There's definitely a difference between the outside appearance we show to the world at large and the 'real me' inside. Of course, the self-talk I hear—both negative and positive—isn't just my own voice. I hear voices from my past as well. My mom and dad's voices, my grandmother's, my friends'—they're all in there. Sometimes it's hard to focus on the positive and to find that quiet place to hear God's 'still small voice.' But, slowly but surely, I'm learning that the real me is the picture that God paints of me."

**—Michelle, New Jersey**
**Born in 1968, mother of one**

"It wasn't until I had three children, and lost most of my brain cells that I realized how much my inner thoughts affect my outer behavior...and how much I need to protect the few coherent thoughts I have. Learning to recognize the lies that get tossed around my brain—at lightning speed—and then taking them to God to hear His Truth has transformed my walk with God."

**—Amy, Georgia**
**Born in 1970, mother of three**

"I've heard a quote which is used over and over in my life: 'When satan (I refuse to give him honor by capitalizing his name) reminds us of our past, we need to remind him of his future.' It's a great way to realize guilt is more DEstructive than CONstructive. That's where we need to conform our thoughts to Jesus' ways so the enemy doesn't have an opportunity to get the foothold."

**—Allison, Florida**
**Born in 1974, mother of two**

# BONUS MATERIAL

## THE "SOCCER MOM" IS HISTORY

Only 9 percent of Generation X mothers describe themselves as soccer moms. Today's young moms are more difficult to classify, given the variety of factors that shape their existence: They have high levels of education, and they married and had children later than their Boomer counterparts. As a consequence, they generated higher percentages of household income before confronting decisions about whether to return to work after having children.[40]

So how do we balance being educated and highly talented with motherhood? Here's how one famous Gen Xer feels about it:

### *READER'S DIGEST* TALKS TO REESE WITHERSPOON (BORN 1976):

*Did you ever guess you'd be so into being a mother?*

**Witherspoon:** It took me a long time to acclimate myself. I was scared to death. I was 23, got home from the hospital and nobody gave me any instructions. My mother had to go back to work, and I didn't know what to do. I was terrified. The first six months were unbelievably difficult. I didn't sleep. Luckily, I had really good friends.

*Is it hard to juggle two show business careers and two kids?*

**Witherspoon:** Surprisingly, not as difficult as it seems. You have to have sort of a "Things will all work out" attitude. We go everywhere, all four of us, together. It's going to change this year a little because Ava's starting real school. But Ryan and I don't work at the same time, so it's not that hard.[41]

Of course, Reese most likely has a personal assistant, a nanny, and a housekeeper (or two) to help. But what about the rest of us? How do we handle the idea of "having so much ability" and "not shortchanging our kids"? Sometimes the real battle may not be choosing to make the sacrifice to spend time with our kids...but rather living with that choice.

# 8 Once in a Lifetime

## Spending Time with Family

***And you may ask yourself...where does that highway go?***

TALKING HEADS, REMAIN IN THE LIGHT, 1980, SIRE RECORDS (USA)

I have good news. There is one thing our generation is doing right. One very *big* thing, an article by Karen Klein affirms:

> Gen X moms and dads are more likely than upwardly mobile Boomer parents to turn their attention from careers to put a greater emphasis on children and household responsibilities.[42]

That's right. Marketers realize that while the buzz phrase for *our* parents was "quality time," Gen Xers don't feel it's enough. We want quality and quantity time. To target us, marketers know family-related goods and services are the *main things* they can count on to get those dollars from our wallets. (For an overwhelming idea of their offerings, just walk through your local mall or toy store!) They know we'll spend our money on these goods and services because of the emphasis we put on kids and family. But they know this for another reason, too. Gen X parents also spend because there's an underlying guilt we can't shake. We feel no matter how much time we give, it's still not enough.

The same article continues, "The Gen X parents are less satisfied with the amount of time they allocate to family—not because they don't like the trade-off, but because they wish they could spend even more time with their kids."

I actually nodded as I read that last sentence. I homeschool my kids, we watch movies together, play board games, I interact with them as they play, we open our home to their friends...yet still there's this nagging feeling deep in my gut that it's not enough.

And you know what? I have a notion you feel the same way. Why? You're reading this book. You want to do your best as a parent. (See, I told you we were more like each other than I first realized.)

Why is this underlying guilt so often the case for Gen Xers? Why are we doing great as parents, but always feel like it's never good enough? Maybe because we have such high expectations for ourselves? Maybe because we realize how important childhood is? Maybe because we desire to live up to God's holy standard? These are good things as long as we realize that striving for them is not the answer.

Accepting them in light of what God has provided for us is.

## Under Pressure

***And love dares you to change our way of caring about ourselves....***

***Queen, with David Bowie, Hot Space, 1982, Hollywood***

God's love, though, is ever and always, eternally present to all who fear him, making everything right for them and their children as they follow his Covenant ways and remember to do whatever he said. (Psalm 103:17–18, *The Message*)

The word *love* here (the Hebrew word *hesed)* is also translated "lovingkindness" (NASB), "steadfast love" (RSV) and "mercy" (KJV). It is used about 250 times in the Old Testament. It means loyal, steadfast, or faithful love, and stresses the idea of a "belonging together" with those involved in the love relationship. According to the Ryrie Study Bible, "In the Old Testament, communion, deliverance, enabling, enlightenment, guidance, forgiveness, hope, praise, preservation are all based on God's *hesed*."[43]

The Greek word for grace, *charis*, parallels this Hebrew word. It means "that which is a free gift."

Okay, okay, I know. This is getting a little technical. But hang with me—this is an important point. God's love (lovingkindness, mercy, grace), according to Psalm 103:17, is eternally present to all who fear him. If we follow His covenant ways and remember to do what He says, He will make everything right for us and our children. (Right as He sees fit, that is, not as we think it should go.)

We can know this truth in our minds, but God wants us to feel it in our hearts.

*Hesed* is possible only through relationship. That makes sense. What good is a merciful God if He has no one to show mercy to? He has made a covenant (which can never be broken) to make everything right as we fear, follow, and obey (which He gives us the ability to do). But in order for the covenant, the relationship, to be complete…we need to accept God's grace, allowing it to be imparted in our hearts and lives.

Our time with our kids is once-in-a-lifetime. How sad it would be if we missed out on the beauty of this journey by living under a burden of self-imparted guilt and dissatisfaction…especially when we have a God who is offering us grace and lovingkindness.

Do not be burdened, my friend. You're doing it right—and will continue to—with the help of God who's made a covenant to help you. God swore by Himself to do so. And that amazes me.

## My Take On It

"I put a lot of pressure on my children to be the best they can be, and I forget that they're just kids and they're supposed to make mistakes. Oftentimes I get frustrated because they're not measuring up to my expectations.

"I spend most of my time parenting, instructing, and yes, yelling that I rarely get the opportunity to enjoy my children. Too many times I have to tell myself to stop and enjoy the moment because it won't last long."

**—Gina, Oklahoma**
**Born in 1968, mother of four**

"I tend to focus on all that I am doing wrong as a parent. Even when people compliment me on what good kids I have, I always respond in a negative way: 'Yeah, when they aren't bickering,' or 'If you only knew.' I know my kids are good kids, but I am constantly aware of my failings as a parent.

"The enemy seeks to destroy. He likes to distort God's truth in order to plant guilt deep into our soul. Guilt and grace cannot coexist. If I am consumed by the burden of guilt, the gift offering of grace is blurred and hard to grasp."

**—Michelle H., Ohio**
**Born in 1971, mother of four**

"Yes! I feel guilty. I do feel like we made the right choice when my husband and I decided that I would be a stay-at-home (okay, work-at-home) mom, and I wouldn't change that decision at all. But I still feel like I was such a productive member of the family back when I was working full-time. Although I know my 'job' now is MUCH harder and much more important, I still can't get rid of this nagging doubt that I'm not pulling my weight because I'm not bringing in a full-time paycheck. So, I find myself feeling guilty if I'm not constantly busy doing mom-type stuff. My working mom friends feel guilty because they are missing all their kids' milestones. It's one of those situations where you just can't win. I suppose I need to just keep viewing myself through God's eyes—trusting Him to lead so that I am right where He wants me to be."

**—Michelle D., New Jersey**
**Born in 1968, mother of one**

## Believe It or Not

***I'm walking on air. I never thought I could feel so free....***

**JOEY SCARBURY, AMERICA'S GREATEST HERO, 1981, COLLECTABLES**

**(THEME SONG FOR THE TV SHOW THE GREATEST AMERICAN HERO)**

As I'm working on this book, my husband, John, and I are praying about the possibility of adopting a baby girl from China. (It's something that's been on my heart for a while...and something we're both now feeling drawn to.)

As I was discussing this with my sixteen-year-old son, I told him, "Your dad and I feel we have more love to give...and we think we're pretty good parents."

A smile brightened Cory's face. "I think it's an awesome idea, because you're not good parents...you're *great* parents."

Instantly, tears sprang to my eyes. Why? His words surprised me. Even though I work really hard to be a good mom...even though I write about parenting...even though my kids are turning out pretty darn good, I spend more time focusing on where I'm lacking than on what I'm doing right. And although I'm writing these words to encourage you to accept God's grace and steadfast love as you parent, it's a message that needs to hit home in my own heart, too.

Charles Spurgeon writes:

> A higher form of faith is that faith which *grows out of love*. Why does a boy trust his father? The reason why the child trusts his father is because he loves him. Blessed and happy are they who have a sweet faith in Jesus, intertwined with deep affection for Him, for this is a restful confidence. These lovers of Jesus are charmed with His character, and delighted with His mission, they are carried away by the lovingkindness that He has manifested, and therefore they cannot help trusting Him, because they so much admire, revere, and love Him.[44]

We are doing an awesome job as a generation of parents, and God wants us to understand what this "restful confidence" is all about. As lovers of Jesus, we are charmed with His character and delighted with His mission. Now He desires for us to be carried away by His lovingkindness. As Spurgeon reminds us, "Therefore they cannot help trusting Him."

Can you get to that place of restful confidence? Not only when you're doing exceptional things as a parent, but also when you're interacting in ordinary, simple ways?

I'll tell you what. If you try to allow yourself to be carried away by His lovingkindness, I'll try, too.

After all, we want to give our kids the best. And *this* truth in our hearts would be it.

> Old habits are hard to break, and no one is easily weaned from his own opinions. But if you rely on your own reasoning and ability rather than on the virtue of submission to Jesus Christ, you will but seldom and slowly attain wisdom. For God wills that we become perfectly obedient to himself, and that we transcend mere reason on the wings of burning love for him.
>
> **—Thomas á Kempis**

## Just the Facts

Lisa Whelchel writes in *Speaking Mom-ese:*

> One of the most memorable and powerful Bible studies I have done is one by T. W. Hunt. After listing the many names and titles of God recorded in the Bible, [Hunt] explains that the name we call someone often identifies our relationship with that person: for example, "daddy" (child), "doctor" (patient), "teacher" (student), and "honey" (lover). He then asks readers to reflect on their own relationship with God and identify the most common role they assume with the Lord.... The last step

is to personalize Psalm 23 from your own perspective, using the relationship you identified as your unique prayer identity to God.[45]

Whelchel goes on to share her personal revision of Psalm 23:

*The Lord is my Daddy,*
*I will be loved and adored.*
*I crawl up into His lap*
*and am safely wrapped in His arms.*
*I lay my head against His heart*
*and find rest for my mind, body, and soul.*
*I learn to trust.*
*I take His hand; He holds mine,*
*and we walk together through my life.*
*Surely I will face fear, hurt,*
*disappointment, and loss,*
*but You are bigger than any*
*ugly monster hiding under my bed.*
*I will not be afraid of the Dark,*
*because You are the Light.*
*I don't even think about tomorrow,*
*what I will eat, wear, or where I will live,*
*because You are my Abba.*
*I don't need to worry;*
*You will take good care of me—*
*I am your little girl!*

*You are the Father of my future,*
*and You have blessings and hope planned for me.*
*You enjoy giving me good gifts.*
*I make You smile when I dance*
*with giddy thanksgiving in Your presence.*[46]

I don't know about you, but reading those words and picturing God in that light make it easy to accept His lovingkindness and grace. I encourage you to read it again; as you do, picture yourself on His big lap. (You dad readers can substitute "I am your little boy" for "I am your little girl.")

Now, while you're sitting there, listen in your heart as God shares what else He thinks you're doing right. Then go to His Word and ask Him to show you His messages there. We already know you're doing a good job spending quality *and* quantity time with your family. But there's more. Close your eyes and listen as God whispers His words of approval.

Trust in God's lovingkindness, even more than those voices that claim you're not doing enough or being enough. God knows differently.

> Because of the LORD's great love we are not consumed, for his compassions never fail. They are new every morning; great is your faithfulness. (Lamentations 3:22–23)

That "great love" is true. Trust in it. Trust in *Him*. Not in part, but completely.

## BONUS MATERIAL

> Today's [Gen Xers] think in "sound bites," "big pictures," and concepts, with an incredible capacity for information gathering. They want to be able to communicate 24/7 (twenty-four hours a day, seven days a week) anywhere in the world. If it's not on the Internet, it doesn't count for Xers.[47]

# 9 Adult Education

## Improving Parenting Skills

***So you got a little education, and a lot of dedication....***

**Hall and Oates, *Greatest Hits: Rock 'n' Soul*, 1983, RCA Records (USA)**

As much as God desires for us to enjoy confidence in the areas we're doing a good job as parents, He's also quick to reveal areas that need work.

I know this from personal experience. In fact, I distinctly remember the point in my parenting journey when God gave me a wake-up call.

I hate to admit it, but for a time I really struggled with anger, and I often swatted my preschooler in frustration. This wasn't the kind of discipline where I sat my son down, identified his disobedience, explained the consequence, and then gave him a spanking on the bottom followed, of course, with a hug and a prayer.

No, I'm talking about situations where Cory would do something wrong (or maybe just something childish), and *whap*...I would administer a quick cuff to the back of his head or a flick to his ear. I wouldn't label it child abuse, but neither was it loving discipline.

I remember clearly the day God showed me I needed to get a handle on my anger. Four-year-old Cory and I were sitting at the table practicing his alphabet when I reached over to brush his bangs back from his forehead. As I lifted my hand, Cory recoiled from me, wincing. My heart broke at his response to my gesture.

*Oh, dear Lord. My poor son…*

He didn't know whether his mom would be flicking him or caressing him, yet at the tender age of four he knew to protect himself just in case.

I pulled Cory onto my lap and hugged him. He most likely didn't have any idea what was happening, but I did. As I held and rocked him, I prayed, *Lord, forgive me. Please help me with my anger problem. Help me be a mother who will discipline correctly and who will show my love twice as much as my anger.*

Laura Ingalls Wilder once wrote, "It is best to be honest and truthful, to make the most of what we have; to be happy with simple pleasures and to be cheerful and have courage when things go wrong."

Hmmm…courage when things go wrong. That's a toughie. Courage to realize my parenting skills need help. Courage to seek my child's forgiveness. Courage to seek God's guidance.

In the case of my out-of-line anger, God used that one incident to highlight the problem. Then with prayer, lots of mess-ups, and God's help, I began to change.

It started by realizing my anger and taking my frustrations to God. God showed me how to walk away, to count to ten, to offer my uptightness to Him, instead of taking it out on my children. And soon these responses became the norm…and the swats and flicks, well, those are now things of the past.

## Slothful Servants

The difficulty comes, though, when sometimes "wrong" is not due to horrible habits and hang-ups. Sometimes we're just lazy. We don't get off our rears and do what we know we're supposed to.

As Oswald Chambers observes in *My Utmost for His Highest*:

> We know something is right, but we try to find excuses for not doing it immediately. If we are to climb to the height God reveals, it can never be done later—it must be done now. And the sacrifice must be worked through our will before we actually perform it.[48]

Small decisions, like whether to pray in the car on the way to school, create patterns over time. They also shape larger decisions to come.

What we choose to do today affects our children's future. But when we don't do what God is asking of us, well, that too is a choice. A choice to disobey.

The good news is that Xers are highly motivated learners who ask lots of questions and want interaction. We like to do our own research. We like to be set on a course to determine for ourselves if it's the right one. We don't mind failing if we learn from the experience.

That's why I feel free to share the fact that sins of omission are just as wrong as sins of commission, because like me you'll cringe and maybe even mutter "ouch." But you'll also pray, seek, and ask God to show you if there's anything you're supposed to do and haven't done.

## My Take On It

"I find it difficult to deal with the anger and verbal abuse I endured as a child. As a parent, I find myself impatient and quick to become angry. I'm constantly fighting my impulse to yell at my daughter, sometimes over small but irritating things. I pray for patience and strength and a renewal of my mind. I've also asked my husband to tell me when I have been impatient. I don't want to continue this behavior in my family."

**—Thresa, California**
**Born in 1977, mother of two**

"One of the most humbling things I have to do is ask my children for forgiveness. I'm supposed to be the parent who gets it right. But honesty and transparency require me to admit when I fail."

**—Cara, Indiana**
**Born in 1974, mother of two**

"I wonder if our generation has a problem with lazy parenting. It seems strange that Xers are so family focused, but also want parenting to come easily. When it doesn't, Xers seem to get discouraged. Is it an Xer tendency to say, 'If I can't do this right then I am not going to do it at all'?

"Are we quitters or fighters? Are we looking for the easy way out or at least the easy way?"

**—Jennifer R., Wisconsin**
**Born in 1969, mother of three**

## Lessons in Love

***I'm not proud, I was wrong, and the truth is hard to take....***

*Level 42, Level Best, 1989, Polydor*

The following are two great quotes from two very wise people, Joyce Meyer and Henry Blackaby:

> How God sees us is not the problem; it is how we see ourselves that keeps us from succeeding. Each of us can succeed at being everything God intends us to be.[49]

> When God called Abraham, He said, "I will make your name great" (Genesis 12:2). That means I will develop your character to match your assignment.[50]

God also has something special and wonderful for us: parenthood. He didn't just see us—notice our awesome gifts, talents, and qualities—and think, *Finally, someone worthy of being a mom/dad.* Instead, when we submit to Him—faults and all—He helps us develop character to meet the assignment.

Which reminds me of another wise statement—made by Jesus, the Word of God and Savior of the world:

> "You did not choose me, but I chose you and appointed you to go and bear fruit—fruit that will last." (John 15:16)

So while the truth is we'll all mess up as parents...and we'll all need a little *Adult Education*, God has made a commitment to craft our character—working on the rough spots when we have the courage to fess up. But that, of course, takes humility. It takes realizing who we are and who God is, then going to Him for help.

> God doesn't call the equipped. He equips the called.
> **–Wellington Boone**

## Truly Humble

So what is humility? Here's a story from Kent Crockett in *Making Today Count for Eternity*:

> A pastor was traveling on a bus down a bumpy road. Seated next to him was a college student who noticed that the minister was reading his Bible. The minister asked, "Are you spiritually ready for the temptations that you will face in college?"
>
> "I don't have a problem with temptation," the young man told the minister. "I have strong willpower."
>
> The minister took a pencil from his pocket and said, "I can make this pencil stand up on the cover of this Bible even though the bus ride is bumpy."

The young man said, "I'll believe it when I see it. I don't think you can do it."

"Look, I'm doing it," he replied as the young man watched.

"Yeah, but you didn't tell me you would hold the pencil up with your hand."

"I didn't have to tell you," the pastor remarked. "Have you ever seen a pencil stand up on its own without someone holding it?"

The minister then let go of the pencil, which instantly fell over. "The only reason you stand," he continued, "is because God is holding you up with His hand."[51]

This reminds me of one of my favorite Scripture verses:

He said to me, "My grace is sufficient for you, for my power is made perfect in weakness." Therefore I will boast all the more gladly about my weaknesses, so that Christ's power may rest on me. That is why, for Christ's sake, I delight in weaknesses, in insults, in hardships, in persecutions, in difficulties. For when I am weak, then I am strong. (2 Corinthians 12:9–10)

When I am weak, God *really* has the opportunity to show His stuff. And, as a mom, I give Him plenty of opportunity to be strong.

Take a good look, friends, at who you were when you got called into this life. I don't see many of "the brightest and the best" among you, not many influential, not many from high-society families. Isn't it obvious that God deliberately chose men and women that the culture overlooks and exploits and abuses, chose these "nobodies" to expose the hollow pretensions of the "somebodies"? That makes it quite clear that none of you can get by with blowing your own horn before God. Everything that we have—right thinking and right living, a clean slate and a fresh start—comes from God by way of Jesus Christ. That's why we have the saying, "If you're going to blow a horn, blow a trumpet for God." (1 Corinthians 1:26–31, *The Message*)

The word *nobodies* here is translated "foolish" in most of the other Bible translations. This word in the Greek means "dull or stupid, heedless, blockhead and absurd."[52] (Just so there's no confusion.)

Yet, like the pencil that cannot stand on its own, God understands how weak we are on this bumpy road, and He holds us up. As 2 Chronicles 16:9 says, "The eyes of the Lord range throughout the earth to strengthen those whose hearts are fully committed to him."

That's me!

### WHERE TO GO FOR ADULT EDUCATION:

MOPS (Mothers of Preschoolers) groups

Moms in Touch groups

Small groups

Personal Bible studies

Sunday school classes

Neighborhood prayer groups

Your spouse and friends

## My Take On It

"I would rather hide from my weaknesses most of the time. It is easier. It is more comfortable. It is safe. But if it keeps me from the glory that God has for me, then let me change. Let me see my weaknesses and failings. Let me stop hiding from them and face them head-on."

**—Michelle H., Ohio**
**Born in 1971, mother of four**

"One of the best ways I figure out how to help myself as a parent is to watch the behavioral patterns of my kids. I watch my son struggle with patience, and then realize how often I am impatient with him. I watch him try to manipulate his sister into getting her to do what he wants, and I realize I do the same thing. Not all his flaws can be laid on my shoulders, but I can definitely see my fingerprints all over him.

"Yet, I also see the good, too. I see how he is kind to people he meets, because I am kind to people I meet. I see him treat his sister fairly, because I treat him fairly. I see him apologize when he's wrong because I apologize when I'm wrong."

**—Rene, Oklahoma**
**Born in 1972, mother of two**

"I remember when I was pregnant being nervous about being a mom. Why? Because I've never been very maternal. I never liked to babysit; I didn't have much patience or interest in other people's children. There you have it—my deep, dark secret. Imagine my surprise when a friend described me as a "mom type"—the classic, maternal image I never thought I was. At first I was shocked, but then I realized that I really have changed. Or more to the point, God has changed me. I still have a long way to go, and there are definitely areas where God's not finished yet, but it's comforting to know that He gives me what I need to succeed in His eyes."

**—Michelle D., New Jersey**
**Born in 1968, mother of one**

"Marriage was one mirror God put in front of me to identify flaws I overlooked. Being a parent has been a second mirror. I see things in my life, reflected by my children, that I want to change. If I weren't a parent, I would probably ignore those flaws. But I have to remember it is only by His grace and His strength that any change is possible."

**—Cara, Indiana**
**Born in 1974, mother of two**

## Take Us Back, God

So where does this leave us?

It leaves me realizing God makes us aware of a problem in our parenting not to burden us with guilt, but because He desires to make our character match His assignment.

The hard part is fessing up and deciding to change. It seems easier to just stay the same. But if you want transformation—if you desire altered attitudes, redeemed responses, and strength to overcome your slothful ways—here's a prayer to pray from *The Book of Uncommon Prayer* by Steven L. Case.

It is written as a responsive prayer, which means one person reads the first part and a group repeats the lines in bold. This is a great prayer to pray with any small group you're a part of. (I guarantee they all have their hang-ups, too.) Or you can read it with your spouse. Or you can pray it by yourself, of course—just between you and God. Just make sure you read it out loud. I don't know about you, but speaking my confessions takes them to a deeper level in my mind and heart.

Oh, and while you're at it, take time to also pray for a solution to these struggles. God didn't bring these problems to your attention just to leave you hanging. He has an answer...He always does.

Forgiveness (Ours)

God, we're here again.
**Take us back, God.**
We wandered off the path again.
**Take us back, God.**
Like we did the last time.
**Take us back, God.**
And the time before that.
**Take us back, God.**
Don't keep a record, God.
**Take us back, God.**
We know the way we're supposed to live.
**Take us back, God.**
Your son told us.
**Take us back, God.**
The Scriptures tell us.
**Take us back, God.**
Your servants tell us.
**Take us back, God.**
And we walk off the path anyway.
**Take us back, God.**
To follow something shiny.
**Take us back, God.**
To follow what we thought would be fun.
**Take us back, God.**
We will kneel down here in the dirt.
**Take us back, God.**
We will pray to You again.
**Take us back, God.**
Make us Your servants.
**Take us back, God.**
Your servants will honor You.
**Take us back, God.**
Amen.[53]

# BONUS MATERIAL

## WHERE FATHERS ARE WHEN THEIR CHILDREN ARE BORN:

***GIs:*** Standing outside in the cold, or at a neighbor's house.

***Silents:*** Waiting at the pub for the phone call, with friends and a pile of cigars.

***Boomers:*** Pacing the hospital corridor outside the delivery room.

***Xers:*** Inside the delivery room, complete with video camera.

***Millennials:*** Setting up the live webcam to broadcast the birth via the Internet to family around the world.[54]

# 10 Automatic Man

## Making Room for Daddy

***He was made to play the part; he's no ordinary man....***

*Michael Sembello, Bossa Nova Hotel, 1983, Warner Brothers Records*

NOTE: This chapter is written for the wives reading this book. Men are welcome to read the following pages, but ladies, this is truly from my heart to yours.

My husband John has a picture frame on his dresser which shows a smiling six-month-old boy. The words carved into the wooden frame say, "Anyone could be a father, but it takes someone special to be Daddy." I gave the framed photo to John after we were engaged. We started dating a few weeks after Cory was born (talk about a unique situation!), and we were married when Cory was nine months old. From the beginning, John chose to be not only a husband, but a father, too. This wonderful guy truly jumped in with both feet.

Today, and two more children later, John is still a great dad. He brings fun and laughter into our home. His life is built upon the strong foundation of God's Word. And I've understood the love of God even more by looking into my husband's eyes.

Okay, enough with the sappy (but true) statements, and on to the truth of the matter. Although I embraced the idea of John as my husband from the beginning, I had a harder time letting him be Cory's dad.

Many moms have the same struggle. We spend the most time with our kids and think we know what's best. We want things done our way, and we're not afraid to tell our husbands which way that is.

Which way to discipline, what should happen at bedtime, how to handle chores, what our kids can and can't eat. Oftentimes there are two people with two different opinions. And sometimes the easiest way for a dad to handle the conflict is to willingly step back and raise his hands in surrender.

Isn't that how our generation was trained to act and react? As young girls we were told to be assertive and independent, to show our power. And the young men...well, they were trained to let us.

> Our value systems are shaped in our first ten years or so of life by our families, our friends, our communities, significant events and the general era in which we were born. The biggest influence on us is our parents and their parenting style is affected by the mores, standards and culture of the day. Even though we are all individuals, and experience unique influences on our developing value systems as we grow up, those of us reading this book have nonetheless all been exposed to them in the context of the twentieth century.[55]

Even though "mom in charge" seems natural, I've learned by experience what we think we want (i.e., control) is actually a conflict of interest. When it came to raising our three kids, I thought I knew best. But after a while, I resented my husband for not taking more of a stand and leaving the work to me.

Have you ever felt that way?

I can't tell you the number of times I prayed for my husband to be the spiritual leader of our home. I also secretly desired to see him interact more with the kids. Then one day as I prayed, I felt God saying, "Well then, step back. Stop trying to run the show and give Me a shot to speak to John's heart."

It was hard, but I began relinquishing control. First one thing, then another. And you know what? As I stepped back, John stepped up to the plate. He started reading Bible stories to the kids at bedtime. He organized their chores. He even encouraged me to call him during the workday when I was having trouble with the kids. And I've been thankful ever since.

I recently happened across this quote from Harmon Killerew:

> My father used to play with my brother and me in the yard. Mother would come out and say, "You're tearing up the grass."
>
> "We're not raising grass," Dad would reply. "We're raising boys."

> **And you know that we treated each of you as a father treats his own children. We pleaded with you, encouraged you, and urged you to live your lives in a way that God would consider worthy. For he called you into his Kingdom to share his glory.**
>
> (1 Thessalonians 2:11–13, NLT)

Dads may do things differently than moms would, but different is okay. No, wait—different is *exactly* how God designed it!

Yeah, God has a plan for dads. And as you will see, Gen X dads are rising to the occasion.

## here are the facts:

- **Gen X Dads are unwilling to sacrifice family or personal time**.

  There is certainly a clash of values between the Boomers and Generation X when it comes to work style. Xers have seen how the Boomers can become addicted to work and find so much fulfillment and meaning from their jobs that they neglect other areas of their lives. Because Xers are unwilling to sacrifice family or personal time for the sake of their jobs, they have divided loyalties and appear to the Boomers to have a lack of commitment or lack of initiative.[56]

- **Gen X Dads do more at home.**

  Today's fathers are less likely to draw a hard-and-fast line between work during the week and family on the weekend. Dads are proud to be involved in the daily lives of their children and are more likely to play a significant role in purchases and activities for their kids.[57]

- **Gen X Dads do not feel money is the most important thing.** Books like *What Should I Do with My Life?* by Po Bronson and *Geeks and Geezers* by Warren G. Bennis and Robert J. Thomas show that Xers do not work merely for money. They want to enjoy the work they're doing. They also work to fund their family-centered lifestyle. Gen Xers do expect a bigger paycheck at an earlier age than the generations that came before them, but they also want to be personally involved in worthy causes and give freely to charities they believe in.

## My Take On It

"I want my boys to have many opportunities in order for them to have choices for their future. I was pushing them hard…right away from me! I had a poor relationship with them despite the fact I was spending as much time as I could with them and for them. Only by getting my relationship right with God in the last year have I been able to change the direction we were headed."

**—Scott, Washington**
**Born in 1968, father of two**

"'I like the way I do things. It works. Why fix what isn't broken?' That is how I feel most of the time. Unfortunately, my children have unknowingly been trained to feel this way as well. Because of it, they do not respect their father like they should. They often question his authority, question his intelligence, and come double-check with me after Dad tells them anything. It is very hard for me to accept that my way isn't the only way. But I see firsthand the damage that it can do to a family."

**—Michelle H., Ohio**
**Born in 1971, mother of four**

"One of the most awesome things lately is that my husband has taken over bedtime duties with the boys. It used to be my job, along with everything else, but when our second child was born, our son made it clear to us that it was Dad's job to put him in bed every night!"

**—Heather, Colorado**
**Born in 1977, mother of two**

## DADDY DUTY

Those statistics encourage me. Today's generation of dads, more than ever, want to be involved in their kids' lives, they really do.

Robert Benson writes:

> Time and attention are the currencies of our age. And most everything in our society—every organization, every institution, everyone with an 800 number and a website—is somewhere right now plotting to get as much of both as they can get.[58]

There are many people, tasks, and desires pulling against a dad's time and energy. To see Gen Xers giving this type of commitment is impressive. As I've learned, sometimes we just need to give fathers a chance to excel in their role.

**Here are seven ways to do just that:**

1. **Respect.** Men want to know they're respected. Nagging, complaining, or contradicting is the opposite of what they need. It's even worse when these things are done in front of others, especially the kids.

   Before you open your mouth, ask yourself, "Are my words respectful?"

   Also, remember body language speaks even louder than words. If you're struggling with how to speak or act, take it to God in prayer. Ask Him how you should handle the situation. Sometimes He'll give you the words, and sometimes He'll ask you to be silent while He works.

2. **Friendship.** It's easy to be nice to our friends, to be concerned for them, to share our hearts with them, to rejoice with them and feel their pain. Our spouses should be our best friend of all. Guard their love and their spirits.

   Robert Benson writes:

   > A friend is called a guardian of love or, as some would have it, a guardian of the spirit itself. Since it is fitting that my friend be a guardian of our mutual love or the guardian of my own spirit so as to reserve all its secrets in faithful silence, let him, as far as he can, cure and endure such defects as he may observe in it; let him rejoice with his friend in his joys and weep with him in his sorrows and feel as his own all that his friend experiences.[59]

3. **Room.** Give Dad room to be Dad. It's okay to discuss concerns and problems together, but don't run the show. Our husbands are our partners, not our puppets. And I guarantee the more connected they feel in the process of parenting, the more connected they'll be with the kids. And isn't that what we all want most?

4. **Praise.** We all want a pat on the back when we're doing something right. Offer your spouse lots of encouragement. Praise what he's doing right. Point out how the kids respond positively to "daddy interaction." And when you see your husband modeling God's love to your kids, point this out, too.

5. **Time.** "The truth is that often we are so actively engaged in our outward journeys that we have little time left to make inner ones at all," continues Benson. Just like moms need a break from family and responsibilities, dads do, too. Every time I encourage my husband to take time for himself, I'm rewarded with a man who is more refreshed and energized. A benefit worth the cost!

6. **Grace.** "Do not judge, or you too will be judged," we read in Matthew 7:1. However, what follows isn't quite as sweet sounding as the first verse:

> "For in the same way you judge others, you will be judged, and with the measure you use, it will be measured to you. Why do you look at the speck of sawdust in your brother's eye and pay no attention to the plank in your own eye? How can you say to your brother, 'Let me take the speck out of your eye,' when all the time there is a plank in your own eye? You hypocrite, first take the plank out of your own eye, and then you will see clearly to remove the speck from your brother's eye." (v. 2–5)

I don't know about you, but I'm great at speck-finding, especially with the person I'm closest to. In *My Utmost for His Highest,* Oswald Chambers writes:

> Every wrong thing that I see in you, God finds in me. Every time I judge, I condemn myself. Stop having a measuring stick for other people. There is always at least one more fact, which we know nothing about, in every person's situation. The first thing

God does is to give us a thorough spiritual cleaning. After that, there is no possibility of pride remaining in us. I have never met a person I could despair of, or lose all hope for, after discerning what lies in me apart from the grace of God.[60]

7. **Love.** Do you know your husband's love language—the way he most feels loved? Some feel loved by spending time with you, and others through special gifts. Some husbands need notes written and tucked away as special treasures. Other husbands feel great if their wives verbalize their feelings.

My husband's love language is touch. I know that when he looks like a wilted weed, my giving him a simple kiss on the neck, caress of his hair, or time of snuggling will perk him right up.

Now take a moment and ponder this. How would your spouse feel if you handed him all of these gifts...respect, friendship, room, praise, time, grace, and love? How would you like to receive them in return? I've found from experience that when I give these gifts, they are returned—not only to me, but to our whole family. Now that's what I call an investment that is worth the effort!

## My Take On It

"My husband and I rearranged our schedules so I can work for a couple of hours after dinner while he spends time with our daughter. It's been great. They get some much needed daddy and daughter time. And, because I need to focus on work, I've had to step back and give him the space to do it his way. It's been a really positive experience for all of us."

**—Michelle D., New Jersey**
**Born in 1968, mother of one**

"I love my husband, respect my husband, and trust him first and foremost with my children. However, I am a stay-at-home mom who just happens to be OCD in the way things are done around here! I need to let my husband do what he thinks is best at times—just let him be the terrific dad he truly is. The bottom line: No one else loves these children or wants as much for them as much as me, except my husband, so I think I can trust him with making a few decisions!"

**—Kristy, Texas**
**Born in 1971, mother of three**

"Getting my husband to take time for himself used to be a huge problem. We have what we've termed Executive Wifely Privilege. This is the practical override my husband knows means NO in no uncertain terms, generally used when he wants a really expensive toy/gadget which is not practical for our budget. I don't use it often and therefore it doesn't get abused. There have been a few times when the EWP has needed to be used to get him out of the house for some time away. Once he realized the break from everything did him good, it became less necessary for me to push him into it. He also became much more understanding of my needing a weekly ladies' night out for coffee. He could see my time away gave me clarity and space to be a better mom and wife."

**—Allison, Florida**
**Born in 1974, mother of two**

# BONUS MATERIAL

## FROM COOL TO CONSERVATIVE

Caroline Overington has studied the differences between Gen Xers and Boomers. She writes in the article "Gen X Keen on the ABCs of Raising Gen Y":

> Married Generation Xers are the most traditional, conservative group in the country. They are much more traditional than their Boomer parents. I think we are seeing a backlash against the Boomers, who raised their kids in an era where there was a lot of divorce. A lot of Gen Xers suffered during that period and they are determined to do it differently for their own kids.[61]

## WHAT ARE GEN XERS BACKLASHING AGAINST?

> A new generation [of boomers] brought new beliefs and new ways, and its impact in the mid-1970s was so notable because that new generation was so large.... The early Boomers witnessed the arrival of television as a common fixture in almost every home. They experienced television's persuasive and often corrosive influences, but not when they were youngsters, not during the years when their outlook on life was being shaped. Younger boomers grew up in the constant presence of television, and the more frequents and more explicit depictions of sex and violence held little shock value for them....
>
> The [baby boom] generation made acceptable what previous generations had rejected. Their attitudes toward sex, marriage, parenting, and divorce generally differed from that of their parents. Many of them viewed the use of drugs less harshly. Although many women regarded it desirable to find a husband or live-in partner in college, unlike most of their mothers they also had careers in mind. The careers might be interrupted by childbearing, but not too soon and not too often.[62]

# 11 Hold On Loosely

## Raising Content Kids

*If you cling too tight, babe, you're gonna lose control....*

.38 Special, *Wild-Eyed Southern Boys*, 1981, *Billboard*

I never considered myself poor as a child until I looked back and compared what my kids have with what I had. Like many Gen Xers in the early '80s, my dad was unemployed for a few years. I didn't really think much about it then. Many of my friends' dads were unemployed, too.

To me, my dad was a silent figure in his La-Z-Boy who was "there" but not really active in my life. Looking back on the situation as an adult, I realize how tough it must have been to not have a job or hope for a solid future.

During the 1979–1982 recession, unemployment rose to 10.8 percent (more than 12 million Americans were out of work). Business bankruptcies rose 50 percent from 1981 to 1982. In June 1982, 584 businesses failed, which came close to the Depression record of 612 in one month in 1932.[63]

Truthfully, just because time has passed doesn't mean the money situation has gotten any easier for today's young families. In fact, I would say money issues are one of the biggest struggles my husband and I have as parents. (Can anyone give me an *amen*?)

## here are the facts:

- The Reach Advisors study found that 46 percent of Generation Xers feel they have less financial security than their parents. In fact, the U.S. General Accounting Office reports the debt levels for Generation Xers are 78 percent higher than they were for baby boomers at comparable ages.

- The Xers have a similar view to that of boomers. They prefer immediate gratification—they just don't have as much discretionary money to spend. They are forced to delay gratification for financial reasons, but they don't feel good about it like the Builders do.[64]

- Generation Xers in the top 5 percent of household income—those with annual incomes of $150,000-plus—tend to be in industries that have seen layoffs and where income growth has stalled. The consequent uncertainty leads to more cautious spending across the entire income spectrum. Where wealthy boomers might brag about how much they pay for something, Gen Xers relish talking about how much they managed to save—and that applies even to those in the top income brackets.[65]

- Gen X parents have more schooling than boomers, yet are far more pessimistic about their financial futures. Gen X parents are more uncomfortable with their debt levels, have much lower expectations of remaining in their current jobs, and are less likely to expect defined-benefit pensions in retirement. The specter of financial insecurity haunts them much more than it did their parents at the same age.[66]

- According to "The Motherhood Study," 88 percent of mothers agree with the statement "money has too much control over our lives," and 86 percent agree that childhood should be a time when children are protected from large parts of the adult world.[67]

That's a lot of confusing—and sometime conflicting—information. We're better educated, yet don't have confidence in our jobs and our future. We feel money has too much control in our lives, yet we struggle with self-gratification like the generations before us. We like to feel as if we're getting a good deal when we purchase an item, yet we have much higher debt loads than generations before us.

No wonder we're a mess! No wonder that money is one of the big topics we struggle with in training up our kids. After all, how can we model good spending and saving habits when we're still learning them ourselves?

## My Take On It

"Growing up made me frugal and conservative with spending, but it has also led me to spoil my kids because I don't want them to go without like I did. My dad rarely paid child support, and my mom had a hard time working with five young children. We had no extra money. We never ate out, never drank soda, we lived off of government food supplements. We had hand-me-down clothes, cheap shoes, and no name brand anything.

"A normal standard of living seems to include many extras nowadays. Cell phones, Internet, cable, and trendy clothing seem to be a need rather than an extra. Also, with the busyness of this culture, dining out is a necessity rather than an extravagance. It is a challenge just to keep up. Stretching the paycheck to meet all the 'needs' of today grows more difficult each day."

**—Michelle H., Ohio**
**Born in 1971, mother of four**

"My biggest struggle is wanting to give my children everything. The best education, exposure to sports and the arts, a healthy social life. My parents divorced when I was six and my mom worked all the time. We didn't have resources for private schools or dance lessons, and when I did play sports my mom couldn't always attend my games. I want to be there for all of my kids in everything they do, and with four kids it's very difficult."

**—Gina, Oklahoma**
**Born in 1968, mother of four**

"This past year God really refocused our hearts on giving His way and putting Him first in our budget and tithing. Within six months we paid off our car loan and that nagging few thousand in credit card debt. Since God refocused things for us, we've been able to model cheerful giving. As a result, my oldest daughter was excited to tell the preschool minister at church about all the things she was giving away to the preschool department. My kids were happy to give from their excess, knowing it would bless others, too."

**—Amy, Georgia**
**Born in 1970, mother of three**

## The Answer

So what's the answer? First of all, in order to teach our kids to "hold on loosely" to the things of this world, we need to model this example. Author Larry Burkett writes in *Great Is Thy Faithfulness*:

> It's not that God wants us to live in poverty; neither does He mean for us to be drawn into the allure of advertising. Our lives should not be characterized by the extravagance and foolish sensualism promoted by the mass media.
>
> We deeply desire something, work for it, finally get it, and shortly thereafter we experience boredom or emptiness. This is why God wants to fulfill the desires of our spirits—because these other desires never can be totally gratified.[68]

The answer to our "overindulgence" problem comes as we continually view wealth in light of Scripture. Everywhere we look, advertisers tell us what we want, need, desire. Yet there's only one place that reminds us where to find true riches.

## Check out these verses:

- "A greedy person is really an idolater who worships the things of this world" (Ephesians 5:5, NLT).
- "I know what it is to be in need, and I know what it is to have plenty. I have learned the secret of being content in any and every situation, whether well fed or hungry, whether living in plenty or in want" (Philippians 4:12).
- "But godliness with contentment is great gain. For we brought nothing into the world, and we can take nothing out of it. But if we have food and clothing, we will be content with that. People who want to get rich fall into temptation and a trap and into many foolish and harmful desires that plunge men into ruin and destruction. For the love of money is a root of all kinds of evil" (1 Timothy 6:6–10).

While these Scripture verses are great reminders concerning the trappings of wealth, another verse speaks to our promised inheritance:

> You know how full of love and kindness our Lord Jesus Christ was. Though he was very rich, yet for your sakes he became poor, so that by his poverty he could make you rich. (2 Corinthians 8:9, NLT)

The word *poor* here literally means "beggar."[69] Jesus, the creator of all we see and have, gave up everything for us to become truly rich. He owned nothing and, in fact, turned His back on the wealth of this world which Satan offered Him. He embraced poverty so that we, in turn, could be ushered into eternity.

So how can we train up our children to understand the difference between true riches and the poor substitutes this world offers?

1. **Control debt.** I will step forward and raise my hand, letting you know this is something John and I struggle with, yet are gaining control over day by day.

   All of us, as Gen Xers, are diligent about so many things in our lives. We devote ourselves to our families. We work hard. We volunteer. We fill up our calendar with good things. And then we pray, "Lord, help us to become self-controlled with our debt"—as if God is going to mysteriously cause us not to desire money and things.

   God will help us, but we have to be willing to heed the Spirit's voice. We have to be willing to sacrifice what we want now for what is best for our families, for eternity.

2. **Model contentment.** "I want this. I need that." I hear it coming out of my kids' mouths and it sounds sooooo familiar. Why? Because it comes out of mine all the time. Yet, when thanksgiving comes out of my mouth instead of discontentment, my kids model this, too.

3. **Glorify God.** Is our purpose to see how much we can obtain here on earth? Not quite. Author Ted Tripp writes in *Shepherding a Child's Heart*:

   > If your objectives are anything other than "Man's chief end is to glorify God and enjoy him forever," you teach your children to function in the culture on its terms.
   >
   > How do we do this? We pander to their desires and wishes. We teach them to find their soul's delight in going places and doing things. We attempt to satisfy their lust for excitement. We fill their young lives with distractions from God. We give them material things and take delight in their delight in possessions. Then we hope that somewhere down the line they will see that a life worth living is found only in knowing and serving God.

> In terms of Godward orientation, we are training them in the idolatry of materialism. In fact, we even feed the idols. Years spent denying the importance of a deep conviction of scriptural truth will not develop into godly piety during adolescence or early adulthood.[70]

*Ouch.*

Those words have caused me to take a step back and evaluate how I'm training my kids to function in our culture. It also makes me realize if I don't deliberately teach my children on God's terms, the world's terms will quickly fill in where I'm lacking.

4. **Tithe first.** No matter how much or how little you have, teach your children the joy of giving 10 percent to God first. The habits they develop in their young lives and hearts will be the building blocks for future giving.

5. **Give generously.**

> Today, greed continues to rear its ugly head at every opportunity. We all struggle with it. I have to remind myself daily that the joys of sacrifice and contentment far outweigh the thrill of a new car or the status of a bigger house. I still tend to measure success in silver, and self-worth by the number of zeros at the end of my paycheck. The rivers of materialism run so deep and rampant throughout society that at times it's all we can do to keep from drowning in it. So what do we do about it? How do we keep our lust for possessions from taking control of us?... The most effective way to overcome greed is to begin using what we have for the good of others.[71]

Give to others in a way that is tangible for kids. We love to participate in Samaritan's Purse after Thanksgiving and in food drives for Christmas. There are dozens of ways families can give all year through.

6. **Read biographies.** The best way for children to understand that true contentment is found inwardly, not outwardly, is by hearing stories about Christians who found satisfaction in Christ even in challenging circumstances. Biographies of Amy Carmichael, Samuel Morse, George Mueller, and John Newton are some of our family's favorites. I guarantee that reading about what others have faced for the cause of Christ makes our lives seem easy and abundant.

7. **Enjoy Jesus.** "I am the Way," says Jesus. No matter where we look, true satisfaction can only be found in Him. Jesus is the true treasure worth more than anything this world has to offer.

   Ask your kids to come up with ways to "enjoy" Him. Sing praise songs and pray throughout the day. Talk about His love, His miracles, and His life. Only this can fill us up and satisfy our hearts! He can do this in a way no "stuff" can.

## My Take On It

"Every night at bedtime our children are asked to list five things they are thankful for. We also teach our children about the needs that exist in this world…hunger, poverty, homelessness. We've had the privilege to take our oldest child to countries in South America and Europe where she could see how fortunate she is. We choose to get involved in charities like Salvation Army, Operation Christmas Shoebox, Angel Trees, and things like that which give her the opportunity to give to others."

**—Stephanie, Ohio**
**Born in 1977, mother of two**

"If we say we value Jesus, and then we buy our children the moon, we have failed our kids. It is hard opposing the world's way. But it is amazing to me how easily my children have dealt with it and have now embraced it—being grateful for good meals on the table, clothes to wear, even hand-me-downs, and really are appreciative when they get a gift that they want. I am grateful that God has not abundantly blessed us financially. We embrace our need and ask God for help. If we had more than what we need I think we would forget to ask."

**—Becca, Indiana**
**Born in 1973, mother of three**

# BONUS MATERIAL

## A SENSE OF BALANCE

### Statement #1

One thing our mothers stressed as children is the importance of taking turns. It seems Gen Xers have heeded our mothers' advice.

> [Gen X as parents] are pioneering a different form of marriage or committed partnership, in which couples don't necessarily both concentrate on their careers, full-time, as their workaholic boomer parents still do. One spouse or partner will concentrate on his/her career while the other studies, or takes on a lower paying job for a while.[72]

### Statement #2

> Xers have brought balance to the forefront of today's workplace. In our survey, when asked, "Which generation is the best at finding work/life balance?" all three generations picked Xers by a landslide. Yet many Xers we've interviewed still complain about bosses who perennially watch the clock and note whether an employee came in a few minutes late or left a few minutes early. "As long as I turn in good work," explained one, "who cares?" This is in part because many Xers (37 percent in our survey) still don't believe they've achieved the level of work/life balance that they are searching for. With so many Xers still searching, we believe they will continue to put pressure on themselves and their employers to find it.[73]

### Statement #3

> Better is the sight of the eyes [the enjoyment of what is available to one] than the cravings of wandering desire. This is also vanity (emptiness, falsity, and futility) and a striving after the wind and a feeding on it! (Ecclesiastes 6:9, AMP)

### Statement #4

> It is useless for you to work so hard from early morning until late at night, anxiously working for food to eat; for God gives rest to his loved ones. (Psalm 127:2, NLT)

Yes, Gen Xers are striving for balance. And with God's help, we can continue to find it.

# 12 WHITE Wedding

## Marriage Matters

***It's a nice day to start again....***

*Billy Idol, Billy Idol, 1982, Chrysalis Records*

Even though I'm only thirty-four years old, I've been married for nearly half of my life. I married John Goyer at age eighteen, a single mother of one.

But this is not a common situation—in fact, I know many Gen Xers who are still looking for "the right one." And there's a good reason.

> For many Xers, the marriage pattern they saw as they were growing up was divorce. That scared them to the degree that they tend to wait longer to get married and are hesitant to get into a marriage situation that could end in divorce. The trend of couples living together without being married (started by the boomers) continues to be a real option in many Xers' minds.[74]

In the article "Gen X Hits Big 4-0," David Athens writes:

> Gen X helped push the average age of first marriage over 27 for men and 25 for women. In 1970, the median age at first marriage was 22.5 years for men, and 20.6 years for women. So far, the divorce rate for Gen X stands at an unusually low 8 percent, but if history is a guide, most would agree it's too early in the marriage cycle of the group to get a proper read on its potential outcome.[75]

In 1980, the divorce rate had grown from one in three (1970) to one in two; one-parent families had increased 50 percent; unmarried couples living together were up 300 percent; and one million teenagers became pregnant, two-thirds of them unmarried.[76]

Like many Gen Xers, I'm a child of divorce. (Okay, I wasn't officially a "child," since my dad informed me he'd filed the divorce papers on my wedding day.) It's sad to note this problem is one of the primary markers of our generation.

Also like many Gen Xers, I'm determined to be married to my husband for life. And because of this vow, I work hard on our relationship. Or at least I think I work hard. There are, of course, always things that get in the way of my being the loving wife my husband deserves…and the main one is life itself.

The older I get, the more I discover the truth behind the old adage, "The squeaky wheel gets the grease." Squeaks come from a variety of sources: kids, friends, church obligations, school, organizations that want us to volunteer our time and talents. Of course, the one usually left out is our spouse.

Letting the marriage relationship slide into neutral is not only bad for us, but also for our kids. We love our spouses, we really do. But, well, they understand life is busy. Right?

# My Take On It

"I choose (notice I said 'choose') to give my husband respect, friendship, grace, and space to be the parent he is. I am at odds with a lot of my fellow female race. I find that I do not have many who find this to be an asset."

**—Becca, Indiana**
**Born in 1973, mother of three**

"Marriage is the core of the family. I'm often reminded that when I experience trouble with my kids, I must remember to check the core, first. Nurturing this keeps the ripples at bay. Now if I could just do this more consistently."

**—Julie, Idaho**
**Born in 1969, mother of two**

"I am a night owl, and I wanted my husband to stay up and talk with me at night. But it's harder for him because he has to work in the morning. So I have started going to bed at the same time he does so I can pray for him every night out loud. After reading John 10:10, I don't want the thief to steal, kill, and destroy my marriage and family."

**—Amy, Montana**
**Born in 1975, mother of four**

"My sister gets up and makes breakfast for her husband every day at 5 a.m. no matter how busy or tired she is. I always thought she was crazy. Or needy. Or maybe she just had more free time, since they didn't have children. I always figure, my husband is a big boy; he can take care of himself. After all, no one is cooking me breakfast or forgoing precious sleep just for me. Looking back, I wish I had seen my sister's point of view years ago. If I had nurtured our marriage then, my husband wouldn't feel so rejected now."

**—Michelle H., Ohio**
**Born in 1971, mother of four**

## All of My Heart

***Remembering, surrendering, remembering that part—all of my heart.***

**ABC, *The Lexicon of Love*, 1983, Mercury**

Even though I grew up in the church, it wasn't until after I dedicated my life to God, as a seventeen-year-old pregnant teen, that I realized attending church and living by rules wasn't what God wanted from me. Instead, my Creator desired a personal, loving relationship.

That's what the Bible is about. A personal God created a world knowing a great price would have to be paid in order for us to enter this relationship He desired. Yet He made a way for our hearts to connect with His through the merits of Jesus Christ.

We humans understand this need. We watch movies about love, sing songs about it, read books on the topic. We also distort it. And as a young teen looking for love in all the wrong places, I mistakenly believed this distortion to be truth. In fact, as I was growing up in the 1970s and '80s, my earliest understanding of how men and women interact came not from the people around me, but from the teen romance novels I devoured and through a daily dose of "true love" shown on the television screen.

Myron A. Marty writes:

> Soap operas attracted 20 million viewers daily, and not just bored housewives and shut-ins. College students were among those hooked on the daily dramas featuring troubled characters in life's continuing crises. As in their earlier days on radio, soaps were typically sponsored by manufacturers of household products. In 1976, television networks carried fourteen daytime soap operas, totaling forty-five hours each week. Those who missed episodes could learn what happened by reading plot summaries in the *Daytime Serials Newsletter*. The shooting of J.R. Ewing in the 1979–80 season cliffhanger of the

> prime-time soap opera, *Dallas,* prompted summerlong speculation on "Who shot J.R.?" An audience of about 83 million tuned in to the show in November 1980, when the culprit was revealed.[77]

Eighty-three million?! It seems I wasn't alone in my fascination with the lives and loves of television characters, which often seemed more real to me than the world in which I lived.

And what did this introduction to "romance and relationships" accomplish in my life and heart?

- Even in my early teens I wanted a boyfriend at all times.
- I thought romance meant sweet words, devotion, and physical contact. After all, that's what I saw and read.
- If I no longer "felt" tingles, I moved on to the next thing. And when I heard Billy Idol singing, "It's a nice day to start again," I didn't think it meant starting over with the person I was dating, but rather moving on to someone new.
- I thought "drama" was part of the price to be paid for finding love. Who's dating who? Who broke up? Who's next?

It's only as the years passed that I've discovered what true love is all about. And I've found it not from a confused and searching world, but through God's Word.

> Make my joy complete by being like-minded, having the same love, being one in spirit and purpose. Do nothing out of selfish ambition or vain conceit, but in humility consider others better than yourselves. Each of you should look not only to your own interests, but also to the interests of others. Your attitude should be the same as that of Christ Jesus. (Philippians 2:2–5)

No small order, is it?

Jesus wants our relationship with Him, in turn, to be made visible in our relationships with others. But I could say that for many years, my marriage was the last place one could see Christ exhibited.

In addition to the lies I believed about heart-pumping romance, I can also say that my parents' marriage was far from healthy or happy. So, at the age of eighteen, I entered into "wedded bliss" for what I could get out of it...instead of what I could give. That attitude carried me along for a while, until additional kids showed up in rapid succession and playing house was no longer fun. Then, I knew something had to change.

Either I had to face the fact our limping-along relationship was all there was...or I had to try something new. Without my husband even knowing it, I attempted the second. I decided to try things God's way, and I began preferring my husband above myself. And, yes, I even preferred him above our kids.

I started by getting up with John as he got ready for work in the morning. It didn't matter if I had a hundred things on my to-do list (which I always did); I decided to make the time to talk with him as he ate his breakfast and prepared for the day ahead.

Then—even if there were kids around my knees screaming for attention—I sent John off with a passionate kiss. Eventually, I started waiting by the window as he drove away, blowing kisses and waving good-bye. It's a ritual I still perform today.

A similar, self-sacrificing ritual would (most of the time) take place in the evening when John returned from work. No matter what I'd dealt with—or what I needed his help with—I'd attempt to make John's first few moments at home pleasant.

A kiss on the lips. Then a smile. "How was your day?" And...I'd really listen to the answer. (It didn't matter if John was talking about computers, and I had no idea what a CPU was, let alone a LAN.) I made a point to show John he mattered.

And you know what? Instead of bucking the system, my kids soon started joining in. Some days there were four smiling faces lined up at the window blowing kisses.

I don't know if John realized the change in my heart and made a similar pact, but there was transformation in his attitude, too. He cuddled more. Asked about my day. Offered to help with the kids. Took me to dinner so we could have more time together.

Your spouse matters because your marriage matters. God, the designer of the family unit, even compares Christ and the church to the marriage relationship. Now, that's serious business! This relationship gives kids stability as well as a happy home. And loving parents show children a picture of God's love and Christ's dedication to His church.

Have my kids picked up these loving attitudes? Well, my sixteen-year-old son, whether he's in public or private, has been known to put an arm around me and plant a big kiss on my cheek…often. My youngest son is starting to pick up the same "habit," learned from the two older men in his life. And my daughter, well…one day she was fiddling with my cell phone, switching all the rings and settings (thirteen-year-olds like to do that). I didn't think much of it until the next day when I flipped the phone open to see "John's Girl" in the place where my name had been.

Yeah, I think my kids are getting the picture. And the best part is they're not only living in a happy, loving home now, but my husband and I are role models for their future relationships.

## My Take On It

"My parents had a strong marriage. While I was growing up they encouraged me to not 'limit' myself to just being a housewife (although that's what my mom did). Although I worked for several years before getting married, I am now happily married...and am a housewife! I also have a strong marriage and am grateful to my parents (and my husband's) for providing fabulous examples."

**—Jenn, New York**
**Born in 1972, mother of one**

"My wife and I are very fortunate in that both set of parents are still married. So we both have excellent role models in our parents for wisdom and advice. We also look to an older couple in our church to seek out advice from. Their wisdom stems not only from their own experiences, but from the Father's heart that resides in them."

**—Bill, Illinois**
**Born in 1968, father of three**

"My parents' divorce left me feeling abandoned by my dad. My mom's remarriage to an abusive, angry man left me feeling abandoned by my mom."

**—Michelle H., Ohio**
**Born in 1971, mother of four**

## Love Is a Battlefield

***Do I stand in your way, or am I the best thing you've had?***

PAT BENATAR, *LIVE FROM EARTH*, 1983, CHRYSALIS RECORDS

I truly believe one of the biggest attacks on our country today is the breakdown of marriage in our society. As John 10:10 tells us, "The thief's purpose is to steal and kill and destroy. My purpose is to give life in all its fullness" (NLT).

The enemy desires to rob us of our vows, kill our love and commitment, and destroy our families. When a marriage breaks up, far more than two people are affected. Other casualties include children, close relatives, friends, church members, and colleagues.

I used to "know" this concept with my mind, but in the past year one of my dearest friends has gone through a divorce, and the pain has hit me heart deep.

Not only that, John and I experienced an attack against our marriage even while I was writing this book. I won't go into details about the other person, but I will say that as I worked hard on this project, engrossed in writing about the importance of faith in parenting, I was contacted by someone from my past whom I haven't spoken to in sixteen years. A flood of emotions came over me that I didn't think existed. And it proved even more that decisions I made during my teen years continue to impact my life.

I immediately sought my husband's support and the accountability of my friends. I also turned to God in prayer and dug into His Word to help battle this temptation. I can honestly say that if I didn't have my loving spouse, my faithful God, and the body of Christ to turn to, I'd still be fighting the battle. And while this type of temptation—a person from my past claiming still to have feelings for me—was not an easy one to face, it proved even more that the enemy of our souls will do anything to tear down a marriage.

If I hadn't sought help to overcome this temptation, not only would John, myself, and our kids have been hurt, but so many others too—my close circle of family and friends, those I attend church and volunteer with, the teen mothers I mentor, and the readers with whom I share my heart through words.

Thankfully, what the enemy meant for evil, God has redeemed for good. Through this experience John and I have devoted ourselves to each other on a deeper level than before. We've confessed lingering hang-ups from our past and are more open about sharing the temptations we face daily. Our marriage has grown stronger because of the struggle.

But sadly, for many this isn't the case.

> Love is patient and kind. Love is not jealous or boastful or proud or rude. Love does not demand its own way. Love is not irritable, and it keeps no record of when it has been wronged. It is never glad about injustice but rejoices whenever the truth wins out. Love never gives up, never loses faith, is always hopeful, and endures through every circumstance. (1 Corinthians 13:4–7, NLT)

Take a moment to pray for each of these things to be exhibited in you… today. Ask God to show you how to display patience, kindness and forgiveness, then move on to the others.

Yes, it will take energy. It will take work. It will mean sometimes saying no to your kids and your packed schedule. But it will be worth it…to you, your spouse, your kids, and your God. After all, can you imagine a more beautiful thing in His sight than your exhibiting true love in a world searching for this very thing?

Gen Xer Candace Cameron, who played D. J. on the television show *Full House*, said in an interview in *Christianity Today:*

> I've never compared what real life would be like to anything on TV or in scripts. What I've known of marriage and married life is just from my mom and dad and other friends and grandparents.[78]

## My Take On It

"I often think about the TV shows I grew up with, and I realize they are a source of my disappointment in my life. Why don't things work like they did on Little House on the Prairie, The Waltons, Family Ties, or The Brady Bunch? Even today, I wonder why my husband and I can't immediately be fine after our arguments, as they are on Everybody Loves Raymond. My husband is quick to remind me (like I don't already know) that their arguments are scripted. Still, I shouldn't let TV shows give me any ideas of how real life is."

**—Stephanie, Missouri**
**Born in 1965, mother of seven**

"My parents divorced when I was still a baby. I totally understand the very deep hurt of a broken home. My husband and I came into our marriage fourteen years ago with an agreement that we would do whatever it takes to make our marriage work, especially after the children came. We started by putting God at the center of our marriage. We have a 'mindset' that our children are NOT going to know divorce—they are going to get two parents who love them and who love each other. After all, it's what we signed up for.

"I want my kids to be in their twenties, thirties, forties, and up seeing their parents still having fun with each other and touching each other. I want them to see that they can have the same thing in their own lives. Just like the song Dolly Parton sang with Ricky Van Shelton, 'Rocking chairs, rocking babies…through the rocking years.' Well, I want to be on the porch with my husband when we are eighty years old, rocking our grandbabies!"

**—Kristy, Texas**
**Born in 1971, mother of three**

## BONUS MATERIAL

The Families and Work Institute, a center that researches the U.S. workforce, reported that 72 percent of mothers with children under 18 are now in the workforce, compared to 47 percent in 1975. For dual-career couples with children under 18, combined weekly work hours have increased from 81 in 1977 to 91 in 2002.

In short, Generation X parents are working longer and trying to fit the rest of their lives into fewer hours each day. To maximize the efficiency of their non-working hours, parents are forced to find new ways of getting old things done.[79]

# 13 Lay Your Hands on Me

## Hands-On Parenting

*I see your face and sense the grace and*
*feel the magic in your touch....*

THE THOMPSON TWINS, HERE'S TO FUTURE DAYS, 1985, BMG

When it comes to parenting, one label Gen Xers are eager to claim is "hands-on."

Xers take their child rearing very seriously, as we can see from the flood of books on the market, guiding them through every single aspect of their child's development. It's interesting to note that these manuals are advocating a somewhat stricter approach than the swinging Boomers handed down. They want hands-on rules as opposed to the hands-off approach of the Boomer parenting style and the "detachment" parenting.[80]

This hands-on approach to parenting is a good thing. In fact, Jesus modeled this type of training through interaction with His disciples.

Even a casual study of the manner in which Jesus prepared the twelve apostles shows us how effectively He adapted His leadership activity

> to the realities of the situation. He instructed them when they were uninformed, directed them when they were confused, prodded them when they were reluctant, and encouraged them when they were down heartened. When they were ready, he allotted them limited tasks and responsibilities and then participated with them, guiding them through their assignments.
>
> Finally, He empowered and commissioned them as apostles.... Jesus observed and understood what His followers needed, and He supplied it. He always interacted with them within the situation and responded appropriately to it. And within three years these obscure Galileans began to change the world.[81]

Did you catch that? Jesus instructed, directed, prodded, and encouraged. He also allotted limited tasks to, participated with, and guided these men. Only then, when He saw they could handle their tasks, did Jesus turn them loose.

What a perfect parenting example for us to follow.

In addition to the patient guidance Jesus provided, He lived out a truth we sometimes don't like to admit: that people are motivated by rewards. The rewards the disciples experienced were often miraculous. They were fed when they were hungry. They were saved from a horrible storm. They were encouraged by Christ's words as He shared kingdom truths.

The idea of rewards is, in fact, something God established.

> So, you see, it is impossible to please God without faith. Anyone who wants to come to him must believe that there is a God and that he rewards those who sincerely seek him. (Hebrews 11:6, NLT)

Here are some additional verses to illustrate this thought:

Afterward the LORD spoke to Abram in a vision and said to him, "Do not be afraid, Abram, for I will protect you, and your reward will be great." (Genesis 15:1, NLT)

Then at last everyone will say, "There truly is a reward for those who live for God; surely there is a God who judges justly here on earth." (Psalm 58:11, NLT)

"And if you give even a cup of cold water to one of the least of my followers, you will surely be rewarded." (Matthew 10:42, NLT)

"God *is* a rewarder of those who diligently seek him," writes Donna Partow in *Standing Firm*. "It's who he is. It's not just something he does.... He cannot NOT reward a diligent seeker."[82]

Just as we should follow Jesus' manner of leadership, so too should we remember to offer rewards for diligence. I'm not talking about cash or "stuff." The disciples received neither. In fact, the type of rewards our children appreciate most come through unexpected surprises, hugs of appreciation, and praise for a job well done.

As Zig Ziglar says, "Words are the most powerful forces in the world. Positive words of love, hope, and encouragement can lift a person to new heights."[83]

## My Take On It

"For me, one of the hardest things is teaching the kids to be morally sound and genuinely nice in a world that is in moral decay and mean as ever. There are very few role models for kids outside their families."

**—Rene, Oklahoma**
**Born in 1972, mother of two**

"I am worn out. I have fallen into the trap of feeling guilty for pulling my children away from their play to help out around the house. And they play into that guilt with their bad attitudes toward work. I see now how I have taught them to be lazy, ungrateful, and selfish. It is time for a change."

**—Michelle H., Ohio**
**Born in 1971, mother of four**

## Lean on Me

***So just call on me, brother, when you need a hand.***

**CLUB NOUVEAU, THE COLLECTION VOL. 1, 1988, LIGHTYEAR**

Hands-on parenting in most families means that mom and dad are available to meet their kids' various needs.

In our family, this term has taken on a different meaning. "Hands-on" does not refer to parents only, but to all of us who share a home as we live and serve together. We believe that since each member of our family shares rewards such as a home, food, and entertainment, they should also share the work.

I have to admit this wasn't the case when I was young. I'm ashamed to admit this, but I grew up with the notion my parents, my mom especially, were available to me 24/7. My only official chore was to keep my bedroom neat—and even then I learned when my room got bad enough, my mom would grow tired of the mess and clean it herself.

I counted on my mom a lot for my social life, too—to pick up my friends or drop me off for sleepovers, to give me rides to games or cheerleading practice, to take me and my friends shopping when we needed things like prom dresses.

I'm sure my mom enjoyed some of these things, especially the shopping trips, but what bothers me even now is how much I *expected* her help without being willing to give anything to our family in return.

My husband, John, grew up with a more balanced understanding of family members working together. With his encouragement, our family adopted a notion we call "family share"—i.e., "the family shares the rewards, so the family shares the work."

Because of family share, I have memories of my almost two-year-old son, Cory, standing on the kitchen counter, putting away plastic bowls and cups as I handed them to him. He learned to set the table at an early age, and even before Cory could read, he knew how to sort and start a load of laundry, using a small angel sticker on the dial as the guide for where to point the arrow for Normal Wash.

Today my teens and preteens have chores that include everyday tasks like loading the dishwasher, putting away leftovers after dinner, and making sure each bathroom is stocked with extra toilet paper. Larger chores include making runs to the dump, taking the car in for regular oil changes, and mowing the lawn. (Teenage boys are, in fact, *very* handy!)

But service, we discovered, is not something that happens only within the four walls of our home.

**Then he said to them, "Whoever welcomes this little child in my name welcomes me; and whoever welcomes me welcomes the one who sent me. For he who is least among you all—he is the greatest."**

**(Luke 9:48)**

We as a family have also taken this hands-on approach to our church, with nine years (so far) spent working in children's ministry. *Wee Ones Worship* (W.O.W.) was born of my husband's desire to start a dynamic children's ministry in our church. In an age of Nintendo and Nickelodeon, John knew that flannel graph and cut-and-paste crafts couldn't compete; we needed to make the Bible come *alive*.

My kids have participated in this ministry since the beginning. They've held squirmy toddlers on their laps. They've acted out Bible stories. They've danced, sung, and acted crazy for the sake of entertainment. And their reward? Smiling faces. Waves from "Wowsters" at Wal-Mart. The joy of seeing children give their hearts to the Lord.

You may be wondering, *So what does this concept of "hands-on" look like for my family?* Here are some basics.

1. **Generously reward teamwork.** I've discovered that rewards aren't bribes as long as we don't use them for manipulation.

   When coming up with rewards, consider what you appreciate. Most of us would tire of work if our paycheck were our only reward. As an author, for example, one of my favorite rewards is getting letters from readers (hint, hint).

   In fact, rewards are most appreciated when they're unexpected: "You've done such a great job keeping up with the dishes this week, so tonight you can go and relax on the sofa with Dad, and I'll clean up."

   Rewards of recognition and compensation lift a family member's spirits and make teamwork fun. Without rewards, family members will be more inclined to get by with only minimal levels of effort.

2. **Cheerfully model a servant-like attitude.** Sometimes I ask myself, am I exhibiting the nature of a servant for my children to emulate? Or do I carry the attitude that the world, my boss, my neighbor, or my spouse *owes* me? Jesus told his disciples:

   > "The greatest among you should be like the youngest, and the one who rules like the one who serves. For who is greater, the one who is at the table or the one who serves? Is it not the one who is at the table? But I am among you as one who serves." (Luke 22:26–27)

3. **Firmly refuse controlling attitudes.** Does your child act as if you owe him or her?

   The perfect example of a child who believed her father was there to serve her was Veruca Salt in *Charlie and the Chocolate Factory*: "I want it now, Daddy. *I want it now!*" I love the film version starring Johnny Depp. When little Veruca attempts to claim her own pet squirrel from the factory, she is pinned down, labeled a "bad nut," then thrown into the incinerator. I couldn't help but cringe at the girl's attitude, mostly because there is a little Veruca inside of each of us, and this blubbering Veruca is most evident amongst those we feel most comfortable around—our family.

   Family members can defuse controlling attitudes by nipping them in the bud. Just as you point out your kids' whines and complaints, give them permission to do the same with yours. Then pray together and seek God's help in gaining new attitudes.
4. **Eagerly embrace "family share."** Families generally subscribe to one of two mindsets regarding sharing. One is seeing how much they can get; the other, how much they can give. Which does your family embrace?

   In order to show our children that families share the work AND rewards, John and I offer financial incentives for our kids. They receive one dollar per year old every month...with bonuses given for extra achievements like doing chores without having to be reminded. We are quick to admit that the amount of money given isn't proportionate to the amount of work completed. Rather, it's another way we've decided to "share" as a family.

5. **Keenly start while your kids are young (or as soon as possible).**

> [By the age of 10] kids move from simply accepting and absorbing the attitudes and behaviors of their families to becoming

> more selective. They hold on to what seems appropriate, but they are also checking out new ideas, attitudes, and values as they are exposed to them through school, media, community groups, and other influences. They are choosing the values and behavior patterns that appeal to them, and they are creating an internal idea of the kind of person they want to be.[84]

Don't wait. The younger kids are when you start building a foundation of morals in their lives, the sooner the mortar will "set." Don't let their peers or television programs mold your children's attitudes and behaviors toward "family." Catch them first to start them right.

**6. Passionately train through double-looping.**

> As a leader who is committed to God's best for your followers, learn well the lesson of double-loop learning. First time around the loop—behavior. Second time around the loop—values and attitudes that drive behavior. Great leaders don't stop after one lap around the loop.[85]

The idea of double-loop learning is a great help to me. I want my kids to understand correct behavior—not to mention the *why* behind it—their first time around. But this concept also helps me understand that it's sometimes enough to work on the behavior first and on my kids' heart-motivation afterward. Just as Rome wasn't built in one day, neither will our kids pick up on moral truths the first time around!

The purpose of hands-on parenting isn't just to make our lives easier as parents. Neither is it to teach our children the concept of working hard solely to reap rewards. Rather, it's training children to join us and our work obediently, in preparation of doing the same for God. As they do this, they are already serving and glorifying God in their lives.

If they obey and serve him, they will spend the rest of their days in prosperity and their years in contentment. (Job 36:11)

Now *that's* what I want for my kids!

## My Take On It

"My fifth-and-sixth-grade teacher had the biggest influence on my life outside my family. She had so much enthusiasm and courage. She had a real passion for the Lord. She had authority but was not demeaning or harsh. She was fun and encouraging. She brought out the best in each of her students and challenged us to do our best in all we did."

**—Michelle H., Ohio**
**Born in 1971, mother of four**

# BONUS MATERIAL

Socialists comment on the strong parental roles in '60s TV shows like **Leave It to Beaver, Little House on the Prairie,** and **Bonanza**, but question what lasting and positive messages were gained from the '90s shows **South Park, Married with Children**, and **The Simpsons**. Bart Simpson is the Xers' most famous cartoon character: irreverent, self-reliant, doesn't care what adults think about him. He's often in trouble but always lands on his feet and usually fixes up the messes of his father—all Xer characteristics. The upside of this, of course, is that Xers are pragmatic, get things done, and don't get bogged down in discussions about discussions. They "just do it," as their Nike apparel often proclaims.[86]

## One Gen Xer's Thoughts:

**PacMan.** Was there life before video games? What did teens do for entertainment before the invention of the video arcade?

**Knight Rider.** Was that a cool show, or what?!

**Star Wars.** Luke was so cute, and all the girls wanted to be Princess Leia. She was beautiful, she was in charge, and she was royalty.

**The Challenger explosion.** What a wake-up call to the nation that we are not immortal.

**Parachute pants.** "But mom…everyone has them!" Everyone, that is, but me. I never was very in style. By the time I got my first pair, the fad had faded.

**Mork and Mindy.** And people think television today is strange….

**"We Are the World."** I still cry when I hear that song. I don't think it did much to change the world, or even bring the world together as one. Still, it was a touching song and musical feat.

**The Love Boat.** Every problem solved in one episode.

**Friendship bracelets.** The popular kids had 20 of them up and down their arm. I had one. I was good at making them, but no one seemed to be willing to repay my efforts.

**MTV.** Even though it was much milder then, it is like taking soft porn and making it available to everyone, young and old alike, in the name of music.

**Gilligan's Island.** What little girl didn't want to be Ginger? Beautiful, exotic…I mean, who could look that good with no shampoo, blow dryer, or curling iron?

**The Beastie Boys.** You've gotta fight for your right to party! Let's just say my morals declined.

**"Where's the Beef?"** I have never before (or since) seen a nation so influenced by a television commercial.

**—Michelle H., Ohio**
**Born in 1971, mother of four**

# 14 Sun Always Shines on TV

## Tackling the Media Monster

*I reached inside myself, and found nothing there....*

A-HA, *HUNTING HIGH AND LOW*, 1985, WARNER BROTHERS

I have a love/hate relationship with my television set. On one hand, I wish we didn't have one (okay, actually four) in our house. If we didn't, we would undoubtedly spend more time talking, interacting, playing board games, and reading books. On the other hand, there are shows I can't imagine missing. Last night our family sat around the tube, enthralled by three first-season episodes of Lost. We were entertained and captivated. And, as a writer, I loved taking note of the characters, dialogue, and plot twists that work—that keep us wanting "just one more episode."

Some of you have quit television cold turkey, and I applaud that. I too want to protect my kids from the media's influence. But I don't think it's possible, or wise, to shun television culture completely. My kids will be bombarded by the media's messages their entire life. Isn't it better to teach them how to make wise decisions concerning their choices of entertainment? Won't it benefit my children to train them to view television, radio, and movies in light of God's truth? I feel like when I was ten and tried to balance myself in the middle of a see-saw: Sometimes I lean more to one side, sometimes the other.

Like it or not, the daily struggle of Gen X parents and their kids includes this draw to all things entertaining, exciting, and broadcasted over airwaves 24/7. Lest you forget, it was that way with our generation, too. Movies and TV showed us how great it was to have cool hair and hot moves. Just think how different your life would be if you grew up without Saturday morning Smurfs or dancing along to Michael Jackson's *Thriller*.

Myron A. Marty writes:

> By the mid-1970s about half of the American households had two or more television sets. The sets had become, in historian Cecelia Tichi's words, the home's "electronic hearth," the focal point in a room. Viewers absorbed their radiating warmth and flickering images. They were also a home's window to the world, as the programs and commercials shaped viewers' needs, interests, habits, and values. Television's manipulated portrayals of reality became indistinguishable from reality itself. "As seen on TV..." validated claims and opinions.[87]

William Strauss and Neil Howe also discuss the media impact on Generation X in their book *Generations: The History of America's Future, 1594 to 2069.* The label Strauss and Howe have chosen to give us is "13ers," for the fact that we're the thirteenth generation of American citizens.

Hopefully most of us have outgrown the hopeless and incorrigible attitudes we modeled (or rather, thought were the height of coolness) in our teen years. Still, we remember the impact television had on us, and we want to make wise choices concerning our kids.

I'm not telling you anything you're not already worried about. According to "The Motherhood Study," 95 percent of mothers wish American culture made it easier to instill positive values in children. Most mothers (87 percent) expressed concern about the influence of advertisements on children and, more generally, the influence of media (88 percent).[88]

As I started writing this book, I asked dozens of Gen Xers about the biggest concern in their children's lives. Here are a few of their responses:

*"The biggest challenge in raising children in today's society is media—not only does media challenge and oppose most of my moral values and beliefs, but because of media, the entire process of the brain is distorted. Media sends the message that entertainment is necessary, that boredom is taboo. Media is the biggest cause of today's problems, not just with making immorality move from tolerated to accepted, and then to expected, but also because it can lead to behavioral issues and hyperactivity.*

*"You would think I am totally anti-TV, but I actually fall into the same trap as other parents, resorting to TV for a little 'break' when I need the kids to be quiet for a few minutes. I see the problem but have yet to do much about it."*

—Michelle H., Ohio, Born in 1971, mother of four

*"It is not only MTV that you have to worry about... most television shows and commercials are using foul language, obscene dress codes, and sex to gain audience members. However, television is not the only place they receive this... there are also the Internet, music, movies, billboards, etc."*

—Rosa, California, Born in 1969, mother of three

*"Boomer parents were noticeably absent from shows from the '80s and '90s: The Outsiders, Beverly Hills: 90210, Saved by the Bell, Breakfast Club. Xers seemed to have been drawn to the idea that they could live their lives without adults as long as they had each other.*

*"Growing up, TV was our friend and constant companion. It made us laugh, cry, love, and hate. It was a distraction from our problems and our realities. It was reliable and seemingly trustworthy. Is it any wonder that today Xer parents are using this dear old friend as a babysitter? I know I do."*

—Jennifer R., Wisconsin, Born in 1969, mother of three

What's a parent to do? I won't provide you with five steps to free your family from the media's grasp. You're the only one who can make the decisions about how much and what kinds of media are right for your family. But I will offer a little food for thought:

1. **Interacting with media provides the same experience as if we acted out those things ourselves.**

> Through the media and other means, the values of our culture are communicated to us in experiential, vivid ways. They impact us. The experiences we've had and the messages we've received while growing up are vividly remembered and experienced as real.... But our faith? Well, our faith is often experienced as unreal, something we simply believe and hope to experience as real when we die, but it doesn't impact us in an experiential, real way right now.
>
> So is it surprising to learn that the faith of most American Christians makes very little practical difference in their lives? In terms of what we *believe*, we differ significantly from non-Christians. But in terms of how we live—what we do with our time, how we spend our money, even our basic moral practices—we differ very little. Where is the radical, transforming power Christians are supposed to be experiencing?[89]

Wow! A lot to consider. Here are the important things:

- Through the media, values and culture are communicated.
- What we see through the media is the same as experiencing it for ourselves.
- We have a hard time experiencing our faith with the same reality as we experience television.

- What we believe as Christians is very different from nonbelievers; yet how we live hardly differs.

2. **Values portrayed in media are often ones we don't promote.**

    The media's increased impact on values is due, in large part, to the increase in their accessibility to children. This has taken much of the control of information out of the hands of parents, churches, and educators. In the past, the influential figures could direct the type and content of information that young people were exposed to. That is no longer true.[90]

    As a parent, I struggle with which shows to let my children watch. Even seemingly harmless ones occasionally have questionable plots. And it's rare to find a program (even cartoons) in which parents are portrayed as anything other than mindless entities who need their children to clue them in.

3. **Tuning in to media diverts kids' attention from God.**

    Hey, kids today are MTV kids! They can't sit still for any length of time. Silence, solitude, prayer, meditation, fasting? All totally lame in the eyes of this generation! Nope, keep 'em busy, active, noisy, and shuttling from one Christian rock concert to another. Fill every moment of your program with something to do—otherwise you'll lose their attention (which would be disastrous, because then they'd have to pay attention to God and their souls).[91]

    What would happen if we cut back on media? Like Mike Yaconelli says, our young people might actually have time to pay attention to their God and their souls.

4. **Instead of helping us appreciate who we are and what we have, media causes discontentment.**

Here's how one Gen X mom put it (can you relate?):

*"I am insecure about my appearance and beauty due to the media's display of popular 'beautiful' women that I could never be.*

*"I am insecure in the quiet because of the constant need for noise and entertainment from my youth.*

*"I am insecure in my worth because I could never afford to keep up with the many fads of my high school years.*

*"I am insecure about my parenting because I had so many conflicting examples in the '80s."*

—Michelle H., Ohio, Born in 1971, mother of four

## With or Without You

***I can't live with or without you....***

U2, *The Joshua Tree*, 1987, Island Records

Okay, now that the danger signs have been laid out, what's a parent to do?

1. Consider your values.

Values are uncompromisable, undebatable truths that drive and direct behavior. They are motivational—they give us reasons why we do things; and they are restrictive—they place boundaries around behavior.[92]

If your kids are old enough, discuss what values you hold dear as a family. Also talk about media choices, weighing the ones that are in line with your values against those that are in conflict with them. I've personally found that sometimes my kids are better at drawing a firm line than I am.

2. **Choose a response for your family and make it known.** Response is unavoidable; either we take a stand or we don't. We ignore, resist or reject God's initiatives and requirements, or we choose to follow them.

> Finally, brothers, whatever is true, whatever is noble, whatever is right, whatever is pure, whatever is lovely, whatever is admirable—if anything is excellent or praiseworthy—think about such things. (Philippians 4:8)

In the past I've written out this verse on a three-by-five-inch card and stuck it to our television set. It's a good guideline to follow.

3. **Ask Jesus what He thinks.** In chapter 2, I shared about how I enjoy escaping throughout the day to seek God's strength. During those times I like to imagine God on His throne, with Jesus at His side. It's a good vision, and one that lifts me up during my stressed-out moments.

But equally important, I feel, is grasping that image and bringing Jesus "down to earth" with me—truly comprehending that Jesus is with me all the time. He's here right now, in the middle of the mess. He's here cruising along with my schedule, my choices, and my world.

John Fischer writes in *Finding God Where You Least Expect Him*:

> If God sees everything, wouldn't you want to know what he thinks about what he sees? I venture to guess he has an opinion; why don't we ask him about that? Do we walk out of a movie and wonder what God thought of it? Do we finish a fine meal and wonder if God liked it? Do we read the paper and wonder what God's take on the news is? Or better yet, do we find him in the news? We need to adopt a way of thinking that puts God within the frame of our daily vision.[93]

No decision is wise if it is made independently of God. What is *He* saying to you about your media choices?

## My Take On It

"It is interesting how today the Entertainment Channel goes back to these TV shows of 'perfect families' and talks about how dysfunctional the people were off set. Does it soothe our own dysfunction by getting joys out of seeing how the perfect Cosby Show wasn't so perfect?"

**—Koryn, Iowa**
**Born in 1978, mother of one**

"I thought TV would be hard to give up. I've discovered only by replacing it with godly things will it make any difference. I do watch movies on the television once in a while, but most of the time I don't have time for it. I've got better things to do. It is a choice for change. Sometimes it can be for better, but we should not be too legalistic about it."

**—Scott, Washington**
**Born in 1968, father of two**

## BONUS MATERIAL

In America the number of children involved in divorces increased by 300 percent in the forty-year period from 1940 to 1980. The divorce boom meant that many an Xer spent every second weekend at their other parent's home, and saw a profusion of different family relationships, such as 'dad's girlfriend,' 'mom's previous ex-husband,' 'my second stepfather', or 'my stepsister's half-brother's mother.' No wonder Xers are skeptical about relationships, yet feel a need to fill the void with something else. That 'else' has turned out to be surrogate families made up of friends and peers who are chosen for their closeness, loyalty and dependable relationships. The result is that Xers often have long-lasting, dedicated friendships that can elude other generations.[94]

Most Gen Xers believe *family* can include any of several different types of relationships. About one out of every four Gen Xers describes family in each of the following ways:

- People with whom you have close relationships or deep personal/emotional bonds (28 percent).
- Those individuals with whom you have a mutual personal commitment or love relationship (25 percent).
- Your good friends; those with whom you are compatible and with whom there is mutual caring (24 percent).
- The people who are there for you to provide help or emotional support as needed (24 percent).
- People who are related by marriage (21 percent).
- Individuals to whom you are closely related, by marriage or blood (19 percent).[95]

# 15

# All over the World

## Creating a Well-Connected Neighborhood

***Everybody got the word....***

*ELO (Electric Light Orchestra), Xanadu, 1980, Jet/MCA*

If you stop by the Goyer house on any given Sunday afternoon, you'll find a unique collection of people we consider "family." In addition to me, my husband, our three kids, and my grandmother who lives with us, hanging out would be a single man in his fifties (one of my husband's best friends), a teen couple and their two children (whom my husband and I are mentoring), and a college student (who comes for the free food and fun atmosphere). Others may come and go depending on the weekend, including relatives that live nearby, but it's this core group you'll find squeezed around the dining room table, chatting in the kitchen, watching a movie in the living room, or sometimes playing board games.

"Community" is something my husband and I cherish. A desire for a close-knit community was one of the reasons we moved from bustling California to the slower pace of Montana. (By the way, this trend of choosing "family-friendly living" over "big salaries" among Gen Xers is being noted by statisticians.)

We also considered community when we decided to build our house (in a neighborhood with many other Christian families), through the ministries we choose, and in our decision to homeschool. Unlike the latchkey existence of my husband's and my childhoods, our three kids interact with a wide variety of people of different ages every day of the year.

Of course, it would be easy for us to cocoon ourselves in a Christian network of likeminded believers. The drive to church takes five minutes, and the classes and sporting teams we sign up for mostly involve other homeschoolers. But, personally, we believe community should include not only those who share the same beliefs and lifestyles, but others who need to hear the good news of Jesus.

I remember the first year I started volunteering with teen mothers at our local crisis pregnancy center. My daughter, Leslie, was ten at the time, and she enthusiastically offered to help watch the babies of the teen mothers. While the environment was "safe" for the most part—Leslie worked with other Christian women—there were times I cringed, wondering what Leslie thought about some of the conversations typical for unmarried teenagers with kids. There was talk about birth control, about what guy was living with which girl, about who was pregnant for the second time.

I clearly remember Leslie's wide eyes when she met one of our teen mothers, just fourteen years old. "Mom, that's not much older than me," she said. "I can't imagine having a kid in a few years."

Needless to say, my daughter and I shared numerous conversations on our drives home from those meetings. We discussed how seemingly small choices (such as whom to date) can affect our whole lives. We discussed God's plan for purity and the heartache caused when we stray from this plan. We discussed mothering, marriage, abortion, and childbirth. We also talked about how we could show the love of Jesus to these hurting girls by loving them as He would.

Looking back, I can see that when I encouraged Leslie to volunteer I didn't fully comprehend the community I was building around our lives. Connection with these young women soon extended beyond Thursday nights; we had young women over for dinner, gave them rides to appointments, made emergency "diaper runs," and played Secret Santa during the Christmas season. Yet I can see this has been a good experience, not only for me and Leslie, but for our whole family. We've all had front-row seats from which to watch the drama of teenage pregnancy unfold before us. We've witnessed the heartbreak experienced by those who still "do their own thing" versus the joy radiating from those who embrace Christ, dedicate their lives to Him, and grow in godliness.

Perhaps you remember the song "All Over the World" by ELO. It's from the soundtrack *Xanadu.* (I know, now you have songs running through your head!) One line of the song goes, "Everybody walkin' down the street, I know a place where we all can meet." In our neck of the woods, the "open door" policy makes these lyrics more than just words to be sung. Gen Xers—and the Millennials coming after us—are relational, remember? We don't believe truth until we see it working.

> The lack of a nurturing environment many experienced as children has led [Gen Xers] to value relationships. Once they get past the difficulty of trusting, they tend to be loyal to those they allow into their lives.[96]

It wasn't until I began writing this chapter that I learned ELO stands for "Electric Light Orchestra." Interesting, since light is what community is all about—asking God's light to invade every part of you, surrounding yourself with the light of Christian friends, and being a light to those walking in darkness...and you don't even have to leave home to do it!

> For the next two years, Paul lived in his own rented house. He welcomed all who visited him, proclaiming the Kingdom of God with all

boldness and teaching about the Lord Jesus Christ. And no one tried to stop him. (Acts 28:30–31, NLT)

The word *boldness* is from the Greek word parrhsia, which means "frankness, bluntness, publicity; by implication, assurance."[97]

I don't know about you, but for me, sitting around my table sharing hot dogs and soda is the easiest place for me to speak freely, openly, and plainly about my faith. It seemed to work that way for Paul, too. Why? As Jesus also showed through His interaction on earth, community isn't about what zip code you reside in or the group of people you attend church with; it's about surrounding yourself with those God has brought into your path.

## My Take On It

"I teach my children that just because these people share our table, it doesn't mean we necessarily share their values (some of which are very different from ours). I teach them that they are meant to teach Jesus' view, and that they are always to think about how He would like them to react."

**—Heather, Colorado**
**Born in 1977, mother of two**

## Walking on Sunshine

***I feel alive, I feel a love,***
***I feel a love that's really real....***

**KATRINA AND THE WAVES, WALKING ON SUNSHINE, 1983, ATTIC**

Of course, inviting community into your home is not the only way to develop a well-connected neighborhood. The other way is to actually, uh, meet the people who live on your street, in your school district, or even through those you connect with in support groups such as MOPS (Mothers of Preschoolers) International.

Robert Wolgemuth tells this story in *The Most Important Place on Earth*:

> As wonderful as my family was when I was a kid, we did not grow up thinking much about our neighborhood. To make my point: One of our family's favorite stories is about the day a huge moving van pulled up in front of our neighbor's house, two doors to the east. The Strandquists were leaving the neighborhood. My dad saw the van and decided to walk over to say good bye. He summoned my brother to go along.
>
> Dad caught Mr. Strandquist as he was walking to his car. "We're sorry to lose you from our neighborhood, Melvin," Dad said with loads of genuine sincerity.
>
> "Aw, thanks, Bob," Mr. Strandquist replied, matching my father's aplomb. "We'll miss you, too." He then looked at my brother and said, "So long, Tom." He smiled and his eyes narrowed, underscoring his genuineness.
>
> My dad and my brother shook Mr. Strandquist's hand and walked back to our house. A few minutes later, as we sat down to the table for dinner they gave us the report of their visit. We would have been impressed except that Mr. Strandquist's first name was Larry, my dad's first name was Sam, and my brother was Ken.[98]

I burst out laughing when I read that exchange, and then I immediately lowered my head with conviction. While I wave at everyone in my neighborhood, chat at homeowners meetings, and take time to visit with a few people during my walks, there are many I don't know...and wouldn't be able tell you their first names if I tried (let alone their kids' names!). But I'm determined to do better—not because of guilt, but because I've seen how God transforms *me* when I reach out to others.

In fact, I can't tell you the number of times I've wanted to stay home from a Teen Mom Support group meeting, or to call our "collected" family members to tell them I need a day off from giving and serving. Yet when I go anyway, open my door anyway—despite the headache and my weariness—God always strengthens me and flows through me. It makes sense after all. Listen to this:

> And may the Lord make your love grow and overflow to each other and to everyone else, just as our love overflows toward you. As a result, Christ will make your hearts strong, blameless, and holy when you stand before God our Father on that day when our Lord Jesus comes with all those who belong to him. (1 Thessalonians 3:12–13, NLT)

As our love grows and overflows, Christ makes our hearts strong, blameless, and holy. Wow! Just like we talked about earlier, in our weakness His strength has a chance to be complete. In our weariness, Jesus in us shines even brighter!

So how about you? What type of community have you created for your children? Have you provided them with opportunities not only to be encouraged by fellow Christians, but also to reach out to others? Is there someone, somewhere that God wants you to bring into your community, your home, or your neighborhood?

When I asked God this question in my prayers this morning, He brought someone into my mind. How about you?

## My Take On It

"Not only do I not know most of my neighbors by name, I couldn't even recognize them if they were standing right next to me at the grocery store. I have done nothing to create a community for my children. They don't even have little friends in the neighborhood. They don't have a neighbor they can turn to in an emergency. They are surrounded by strangers. And it is no one's fault but my own."

**—Michelle H., Ohio**
**Born in 1971, mother of four**

"I have no problem making good acquaintances, but it takes me a while to really trust someone enough to consider them a 'friend' and open up to show myself to them. But once I do reach that point, these are the people I've stuck with over the years. Although we may be separated geographically, there's a closeness and a loyalty that remains."

**—Michelle D., New Jersey**
**Born in 1968, mother of one**

## Running in the Family

***We only see so far 'cause we all have our daddy's eyes.***

*Level 42, Level Best, 1989, Polydor*

Of course, we can't forget the number one place God calls us to experience community—the church. "Our relationship with God is personal, but it was never meant to be private," write Henry and Melvin Blackaby, authors of *Experiencing God Together*.[99] They continue:

> The most convincing evidence that we have received the gift of salvation is that we demonstrate Christlike love to other believers. We can

> claim to love God all we want, but if we are not intimately connected to the people of God, we are deceiving ourselves. First John 3:14 states, "We know that we have passed from death to life because we love our brothers. The one who does not love remains in death." Do you recognize how seriously God takes your relationship with other believers? Have you made the connection? Would you pass God's test?[100]

I am blessed to be part of a great body of believers in our hometown. My heart swells with joy to witness their interaction and their love for each other, and for me and my family. Unfortunately, Gen Xers tend to believe they can "serve God in their own way" without being part of a local church body.

Remember the statistic from the introduction? According to George Barna, only 28 percent of Gen Xers (ages 20–37) attend church compared, to 51 percent of Builders (58+). Yet a *Newsweek* article reveals that "81 percent of Gen X mothers and 78 percent of fathers say they plan eventually to send their young child to Sunday school or some other kind of religious training."

If you're part of the 82 percent of Gen Xers that *don't* attend church, I urge you to give it a shot. Just as our children were born into a family to be loved, nurtured, and supported, so are we as Christians born into the body of Christ for the same purpose.

The Blackabys continue:

> It would be tragic for people to receive the riches of the gospel, and then live as spiritual paupers; to accept such a great love from Christ, and then resent what He asks in return.[101]

What is God asking of you in return? To open your home? To reach out to your neighbors? To seek out a Bible-believing church? Do it. For yourself, for your family, for God. You will never regret sharing so great a love.

## My Take On It

"It seems hard to make time to have people over or go visiting, especially with little children, but we are working to be more involved with our homeschool group. We're also taking the risk and asking coworkers to get together outside my husband's work.

"It's a slow process. People seem cautious about investing their lives in growing a friendship. But I'm discovering that the more we follow the Lord's lead in this area, the more God works in our hearts and expands our ability to share His love with others."

**—Amy, Georgia**
**Born in 1970, mother of three**

## BONUS MATERIAL

By the 1980s the United States had reached what philosopher Albert Borgman calls a "postmodern divide." Beliefs and behaviors of modern times yielded to new beliefs and behaviors. A framework calling attention to contrasts between modern and postmodern beliefs and behaviors, admittedly stated in extreme terms, helps us understand the changes.

In modern times, progress was an overriding goal. On the postmodern side of the divide, progress is not always seen as attainable or even desirable. Sometimes we pay too high a price for it, as when it destroys the environment. The belief that reason leads to the best solutions has yielded to notions that decisions should be made in one's heart as well as in one's head. Where science was seen as the way to truth, other avenues became plausible. The certainties of modern times have been matched by a tolerance of ambiguities.[102]

# 16

# Big Love

## And the Greatest of These Is Love

***Oh, I'll build you a kingdom in the house on the hill....***

*Fleetwood Mac, Tango in the Night, 1987, Warner Brothers Records*

According to The Motherhood Study, at the core of mothers' powerful feelings appears to be a new and intense kind of love women experience when they become mothers. More than 93 percent of mothers responding to the survey said the love they feel for their children is unlike any other love they have experienced. And nearly 81 percent said mothering is the most important thing they do.

I understand this feeling completely. Even though I was only seventeen when my oldest son was born, when I held my baby in my arms, I experienced emotion greater than I had ever known. The same was true for his sister and brother to follow. There's no denying it...I was, I still am, smitten with these kids. I can't imagine life without them.

Jenn Doucette writes in *The Velveteen Mommy*:

> Sometimes I even daydream about what it would be like to live a life of leisure all the time: meeting girlfriends for coffee whenever I want, having time to read a book cover to cover, or even seeing a full-length

feature film. But as appealing as that sounds, in my heart I know something would be missing. I might enjoy having all that time to myself, but then I wouldn't have the joys and lessons my children bring every day. I would rather be like the Velveteen Rabbit—worn-out but well loved.[103]

## My Take On It

"I think the biggest message of hope for my children, as well as myself, is from John 3:16: 'For God so loved the world…' It doesn't get any better than that. It's just amazing to feel that loved for both me and my children."

**—Shannon, Colorado**
**Born in 1971, mother of two**

"At church this week I had two children Velcroed to my side, and I wanted to scream. I should treasure this time my children want to be with me, but at the same time it makes me wonder if I'm somehow failing as a mother. Why do they feel the need to be glued to my side? Should I spend more time with them? Am I not giving them enough focused attention? Ah, the angst!"

**—Cara, Indiana**
**Born in 1974, mother of two**

## Real Love

***We'd trade it all right now, for just one minute of real love....***

*The Doobie Brothers, One Step Closer, 1981, Warner Brothers*

With so many notions out there about what love is and what it isn't, I thought we'd look at a few of the things that we face on our parenting journey.

**1. Our need for love.**

The authors of *Mind the Gap* write:

> Much of the behavior of Generation X is as a result of this often subconscious need to be loved. This generation is starved of genuine love, and will do anything in their quest to find it. They are not asking, "What must I do to be saved?" They are asking, "What must I do to be loved?" They are looking for a safe place, where they can feel important and where they can be loved.[104]

I can agree with this statement completely. At age seventeen I'd tried love the world's way and ended up pregnant, scared, and alone. It was then I turned to God, seeking true love. As I considered dedicating my life to God, I wasn't so much concerned with eternal damnation (although it crossed my mind); rather, I longed for the love and acceptance I'd found nowhere else on earth.

I'm still working on the reality of God's love seventeen years later. As someone who grew up with the notion that hard work equals acceptance, God has worked on reminding me that His love *is* unconditional...even when I can't feel it at times. Over the years, He has peeled back layers of self-condemnation and low self-esteem, until I can honestly repeat these words and believe them:

> I'm absolutely convinced that nothing—nothing living or dead, angelic or demonic, today or tomorrow, high or low, thinkable or unthinkable—absolutely nothing can get between us and God's love because of the way that Jesus our Master has embraced us. (Romans 8:38–39, *The Message*)

And it's only having this confidence in God's love for me, that I can truly love my kids as God requires.

**2. Loving kids through discipline.**

I love my kids. I treat them with respect. I pray for them. I encourage them. I sacrifice my time, dreams, and goals for them. And I discipline them.

For years I had a hard time relating discipline to love. When I disciplined my kids I felt like a big, bad bully rather than a loving, caring mother…until I understood God's view of it:

> "I will give them singleness of heart and action, so that they will always fear me for their own good and the good of their children after them. I will make an everlasting covenant with them: I will never stop doing good to them, and I will inspire them to fear me, so that they will never turn away from me." (Jeremiah 32:39–40)

Throughout the book of Jeremiah, God shares how He shows love to His people: 1) making an everlasting covenant, 2) never stopping doing good, and 3) inspiring them to fear Him so they won't turn away.

God wants us to fear Him so we won't turn away. Yet it seems this very idea of fear is something many Christians struggle with.

Henry and Melvin Blackaby write:

> What we need more than any other time in human history is to fear the Lord our God. To lose the fear of God is to lose the fear of sin. To lose the fear of sin is to lose the relationship with God. Don't let anybody tell you that "to fear the Lord" just means to have an "awe" of Him…. We may choose to play games with God, but "the fear of the Lord" indicates that God is not playing games with us.[105]

Having a holy fear of God keeps us on the right track. Likewise, the loving thing to do is to teach this "fear" to our children by giving them consequences for wrong actions. Without consequences, our kids will not have an understanding of sin. Without an understanding of sin, our kids will have no need of salvation from God. If we ignore their offenses, they will assume God will ignore them, too.

While we Gen Xers know this, we have a hard time following through, especially because it runs contrary to the way we were raised.

> Even when Boomer parents were at home, they tended to have a "hands-off" approach as a direct consequence of the overly strict and protective line taken by their own parents. To avoid being as dominating or controlling as their parents had been, they swung the pendulum and became permissive, putting too few boundaries in place for their children.[106]

Knowing this, my husband and I have worked hard to develop a system for effective discipline in our home. A few things we insist on are:

- **First-time obedience.** No dawdling, no arguing, just obeying.
- **Firm consequences for disobedience.** These consequences have changed as our children have grown older, yet the most important thing remains the same—our kids are aware of the cost of disobedience and they have been assured, time and time again, of our consistency in following through.
- **Presenting a unified front.** My husband and I discuss consequences together and stand by each other's decisions—even if we don't agree 100 percent. Our kids realize this and know not to play one parent against the other.

Of course, parental discipline not only points out offenses; it also encourages children in the concept of self-discipline. Robert Wolgemuth writes:

> Sowing acts of discipline creates a harvest of self-discipline. Or as your coach used to say when he ordered your squad to take another lap, "No pain, no gain."[107]

Of course, pain here doesn't have to mean spankings—although that is used effectively in many families. Rather, pain is any undesired consequence that will make a child *not* want to repeat the offense.

Wolgemuth continues:

> Your child is not looking for another household friend. You're not his chum, you're his parent. And although he will not be able to verbalize this until he's at least your age, what he *is* looking for is your leadership: dispensed fairly, swiftly, and lovingly.[108]

Fairly, swiftly, lovingly. I like that. And as a Gen Xer who grew up with one parent who was more like a "friend," I truly realize the importance of all three. My kids will have many friends. But I'm their only mom. And that's pretty special.

## My Take On It

"Gen Xers are so relationship oriented. Does this affect how we discipline? Kids seem to be more out of control than ever and parents more involved than ever, but structured discipline seems to be less popular than ever. Are Gen X parents too loving? Do they want to be loved so badly in return that they are willing to sacrifice sound parenting to be approved of by their kids? These are questions I have to ask."

**—Heidi, Minnesota**
**Born in 1975, mother of two**

**3. Loving kids through touch.**

Of course, being a disciplinarian alone will not show our love. Discipline must be balanced with loving touch. Gary Smalley and John Trent write in *The Blessing*:

> For children, things become real when they are touched. Have you ever been to Disneyland and seen the look on the little child's face when he or she comes face-to-face with a person dressed like Goofy or Donald Duck? Even if the child is initially fearful, soon he or she will want to reach out and touch the Disney character....
>
> Touching a child on the shoulder when he or she walks in front of you; holding hands with your spouse when you wait in line; stopping for a moment to ruffle someone's hair—all these small acts can change how you are viewed by others. A ten-minute bear hug is not the only way to give another person the blessing. At times, the *smallest* act of touch can be a vehicle for communicating love and personal acceptance.[109]

As I think back on my own childhood, I remember specific times of feeling loved—curling to my grandma's side to take a nap, bouncing on my grandpa's knee, feeling my mom's hand on my shoulder when I had a bad day.

The older I get, the more I realize that love is more than just a feeling; it is an action. My heart swelled with overwhelming love when my child was born, yet the love became real as I acted it out on a daily basis.

Also true is the fact that we can *do* a lot for people, but it means nothing without love behind it.

"Without love, the outward work is of no value," wrote Thomas á Kempis, "but whatever is done out of love, be it ever so little, is wholly fruitful. For God regards the greatness of love that prompts a man, rather than the greatness of achievement."

> If I could speak in any language in heaven or on earth but didn't love others, I would only be making meaningless noise like a loud gong or a clanging cymbal. If I had the gift of prophecy, and if I knew all the mysteries of the future and knew everything about everything, but didn't love others, what good would I be? And if I had the gift of faith so that I could speak to a mountain and make it move, without love I would be no good to anybody. If I gave everything I have to the poor and even sacrificed my body, I could boast about it; but if I didn't love others, I would be of no value whatsoever. There are three things that will endure—faith, hope, and love—and the greatest of these is love. (1 Corinthians 13:1–3, 13, NLT)

How are you doing when it comes to big love in your life? Are you feeling loved? Are you showing true love to your kids through discipline *and* through touch?

Love is an easy thing to talk about, but a hard thing to live out. If you're struggling with this issue, ask God to show you how to accept love...and how to give it. I promise He'll be faithful to show you. He's the one that created love, after all. And He's the one who lived it out and died to prove it.

## My Take On It

"I've heard, and I firmly believe, that kids who are disciplined by loving parents actually feel more loved than kids who aren't. So, when we let the discipline slide, thinking it somehow is a way to be nicer to our kids, or because we feel sorry for them, it is actually less loving. This has helped me.

"Also, God calls us to raise our children in Him. If my child calls me 'freakin' mama!' (which he has a few times) and I let it go, I have disobeyed God's call to teach him the biblical law to honor his parents. Plus, I have not shown my child the ways of God."

**—Ocieanna, Washington**
**Born in 1968, mother of four**

"My parents were very 'untouchable.' Yeah, they loved me and I knew it, but it would have been nice to hear the words and to feel their loving touch.

"I remember once as a teenager, in church, our pastor told us to turn to the person next to us and tell them that we loved them. I was so incredibly embarrassed! My dad was the only one next to me. We looked at each other and just stared at each other, red-faced and horrified. It seemed like ten minutes of silence. We never said it...only stared. Sad. That has always been something that has driven me as a parent to show my love and touch my children. It doesn't come naturally. I have to work to do it."

**—Stephanie, Missouri**
**Born in 1965, mother of seven**

## BONUS MATERIAL

A highlight reel of the leading influences during the Xers' formative years would include such disparate characters as the Brat Pack, Bill Clinton, Bill Gates, Monica Lewinsky, the Ayatollah Khomeini, Ted Bundy, Al Bundy, Beavis and Butt-Head, the Menendez brothers, Quentin Tarantino, Clarence Thomas, Newt Gingrich, O. J. Simpson, **Dilbert,** Dennis Rodman, supermodels, Madonna, and Michael Jordan. It's no wonder so many millions of Xers wanted to "be like Mike"—they didn't have too many other heroes to emulate. With the explosion of twenty-four-hour media and tabloid journalism, Xers saw almost every role model of their time indicted or exposed as someone far too human to be a hero. Where were John Wayne, Roy Rogers and Dale Evans, or Walter Cronkite for this generation?[110]

# 17 You Might Think

## Teaching Values in an "Anything Goes" Culture

***I'm crazy, to hang around with you....***

THE CARS, *HEARTBEAT CITY*, 1984, ELEKTRA ENTERTAINMENT

Okay, I admit it: Sometimes "anything goes" seems appealing.

"Anything goes" is easy and accessible. It takes no energy. It caters to my flesh. *People* magazine calls to me from the magazine rack next to the checkout stand. Google tempts me to enter the name of an old flame "for curiosity's sake." Reruns of *Friends* don't seem as bad when nothing else is on. After all, the kids are in bed, and I just want to veg out.

The struggle comes when I refuse to give in. Refuse to fall to temptation, despite the fact that the high road seems neither as accessible nor as fun.

In 1984, the song "You Might Think" hit #7 on the charts. "Though you think I'm crazy or foolish," Rick Ocasek sang, "all I want is you."

Those words remind me of what I *do* want most of all...and that is God. And choosing God means turning my back to "anything goes." It's denying flesh for the sake of faith.

Isaiah 32:8 says, "The noble man makes noble plans, and by noble deeds he stands." That word *noble* got me thinking (maybe because it's used three times in this verse?). Just what does it mean, and how can we achieve it?

The Hebrew word for *noble* comes from the root word nâdab, which means "to volunteer or present oneself willingly." Likewise, the phrase "makes noble plans" refers to being "deliberate or resolved" in our decisions.[111]

Wow! To be a noble woman, I need to be willing hearted, *volunteering my will* to God. It's not about what I want or what is easiest. It's turning my desires over to God and following Him. Only then can I be *deliberate or resolved* in the plans God has for me.

I don't know about you, but bending my will to God's isn't always easy. It means trusting without seeing, and hoping without evidence things *will* turn out all right.

The fact is, sometimes I *want* to volunteer but don't have the strength or the resolve to do so. Thankfully, God understands. In Mark 9:24 we read about a father who desired his son's healing.

> Immediately the boy's father exclaimed, "I do believe; help me overcome my unbelief!"

You know what? Jesus honored that. Jesus didn't say, "Sorry, you don't have enough faith so I'm not going to help." Instead, he commanded the deaf and mute spirit to leave the boy. It gives me hope that God honors our prayers, even when we need help praying them.

After all, having this willingness to follow the high road ourselves is the only way we'll be able to demand the same of our children. We can't instill values that we don't hold dear ourselves. We can't raise noble children, when we don't strive after it in our own lives.

*Lord, I want to be willing to choose Your plans over my own. I desire Your values to rule my life and heart...help my unwillingness!*

## My Take On It

"Integrity is doing the same thing regardless of whether anyone is watching. Consistency is doing the right thing regardless of whether I get any benefit from somebody noticing. If I can live that and my kids can catch it, I will have been a success."

**—Cara, Indiana**
**Born in 1974, mother of two**

"I struggle with trusting God. I truly cry out, 'Lord, help me in my unbelief!' I'm not there yet. In fact, lately I have found myself having to obey God's Word and not truly understanding why or feeling like it. The understanding usually comes later, but not always. That is a truth I have been able to talk to my children about."

**—Scott, Washington**
**Born in 1968, father of two**

## Something to Believe In

***Oh, Lord arise, and give me something to believe in . . .***

POISON, *FLESH AND BLOOD*, 1990, CAPITOL RECORDS

When it comes to instilling values in our children, we sometimes feel incompetent. After all, we're so lacking ourselves. The challenge is that values aren't something imbedded in us from the moment we ask Jesus into our hearts. Instead, as we submit to God's way, it becomes *our way*. Brick by brick, truth by truth, we build within our hearts (and our resolve) something called "moral character." God instills His values in us, assisting us at every step, until we can claim these values as our own.

> Values are what we believe to be right or wrong, good or bad, worthy or unworthy. What we value is what we feel is worth fighting for or standing up for. It is what we believe in. Our values guide our lives. They give us direction, are a basis for decision-making, and help us make choices. Our lives are not just controlled by circumstances, habits, emotions, or random occurrences. Our values have a significant impact on all that we do and think.[112]

Values, then, should not only be something we believe, but something we live...no matter how much easier the alternative is.

> People let us down again and again, because there is often a discrepancy between what they claim and what they live. The biblical virtue of integrity points to a consistency between what is inside and what is outside, between belief and behavior, our words and our ways, our attitudes and our actions, our values and our practice....
>
> Whether you're in charge of a multi-million-dollar business or a two-year-old child, manage your affairs with honesty. Let your personal commitment to integrity show in what you do during the day, every day.[113]

We talked earlier about modeling the behavior/values we desire our children to develop. The only way to do that is to allow God to line us up according to *His* measuring stick.

Sometimes God's messages are easy to digest. Other times they seem harsh, such as this following passage:

> You didn't think, did you, that just by pointing your finger at others you would distract God from seeing all your misdoings and from coming down on you hard? Or did you think that because he's such a nice God, he'd let you off the hook? Better think this one through from the beginning. God is kind, but he's not soft. In kindness he takes us firmly by the hand and leads us into a radical life-change...

If you go against the grain, you get splinters, regardless of which neighborhood you're from, what your parents taught you, what schools you attended. But if you embrace the way God does things, there are wonderful payoffs, again without regard to where you are from or how you were brought up. (Romans 2:3–4, 9–10, *The Message*)

This is a message for us as parents (and as people). It's also a message for our kids. Values, we need to remind our children, aren't things that we pick and choose from among the many offered by society. Instead, they develop within us when we submit to God's way of thinking, living nobly by His standards.

## My Take On It

"I saw a sign on a church once that said, 'Raising G-rated kids in an R-rated world.' That's the challenge I'm facing with three daughters. The pop idol teenage images Hollywood and the media push aren't the ideal role models for young girls, and yet the social pressure is everywhere you look."

**—Bill, Illinois**
**Born in 1969, father of three**

"I struggle greatly with laziness. Not the kind of laziness that Peg Bundy showed (sitting on the couch eating bon-bons all day)—I work hard for a living. But when it comes to making decisions and choices about how I parent and how I live my life, I often take the easy road. The high road is just too much work."

**—Michelle H., Ohio**
**Born in 1971, mother of four**

"My biggest concern as a father is teaching clear, biblical-based values in a modern society that seems to shun concrete ideas and the 'rigid inflexibility and condemnation' that they believe is Christianity. Society believes every decision is open to situational ethics based on their desires or friends, not morals."

**—Louis, California**
**Born in 1969, father of three**

## Live It, Teach It

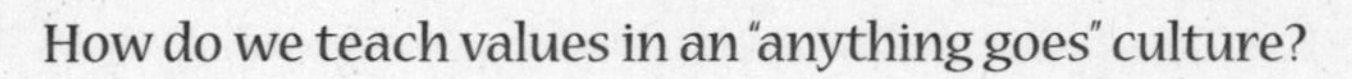

How do we teach values in an "anything goes" culture?

1. **Live it.**

> If you will give God your right to yourself, He will make a holy experiment out of you. God's experiments always succeed.[114]

I like Oswald Chambers's concept here of a "holy experiment." God *does* know what He's doing. He knows what's best for our individual lives, and He loves us completely. Why shouldn't we trust Him and live as He leads?

2. **Use God's Word as the foundation.** Help your kids filter through the many voices by discovering the truth of God's Word.

> Even if it was written in Scripture long ago, you can be sure it's written for *us*. God wants the combination of his steady, constant calling and warm, personal counsel in Scripture to come to characterize *us*, keeping us alert for whatever he will do next. (Romans 15:4, *The Message*)

3. **Share your mistakes...and the lessons you learned.**

> [For Gen Xers] sex education was unabashedly value-neutral, empty houses provided easy trysting spots, and their parents were, as Ellen Goodman describes them, "equally uncomfortable with notions that sex is evil and sex is groovy." ...As Redlands College's Kim Blum puts it, "the sexual revolution is over, and everybody lost."[115]

Sexual sin might not be in your past, but I'm sure there are other regrets you have. Instead of hiding them, hoping your kids don't find out, share your past mistakes (in general terms) and the forgiveness you found in Christ. Then, through your example, your kids will have a better understanding as to why values are important.

## My Take On It

"I remember, during my senior year, learning about AIDS because of Rock Hudson, homosexuality because of Boy George, and discovering that Brooke Shields didn't let anything come between her and her Calvins. To me it was a 'sexual revolution.' It was 'okay' to be promiscuous because that made me feel it wasn't okay to not be."

**—Ann, Texas**
**Born in 1965, mother of three**

"I loved Duran Duran, Lionel Richie, Cyndi Lauper, and the Brat Pack actors. I loved the movies and songs that spoke to the inner pain and quest for a better life than what I had at the present. I think they influenced me to try new things and not be afraid to take risks. Only problem with that was I don't remember any of them having any Christian leanings, and most of the things I tried weren't things that honored God or myself."

**—Amy, Georgia**
**Born in 1970, mother of three**

4. **Compare the world's way with God's way.** Which one truly leads to "freedom": the way of God, or the way of the world? The world says that teens should be free to make their own decisions about their bodies, but how freeing are these choices?

   Sex leads to bonding with another person—who most likely won't be around for the long haul. It means the possibility of STDs, teen pregnancy, and emotional pain. Then there are drugs and alcohol. Do these provide freedom? Not quite, especially when a dependence on a substance leads to lying, stealing, and destruction. A needy user is far from free.

> This "foolish" plan of God is far wiser than the wisest of human plans, and God's weakness is far stronger than the greatest of human strength. (1 Corinthians 1:25, NLT)

Take time to discuss with your kids how God's way is the wise way.

### 5. Encourage your kids to consider what God thinks.

> Don't copy the behavior and customs of this world, but let God transform you into a new person by changing the way you think. Then you will know what God wants you to do, and you will know how good and pleasing and perfect his will really is. (Romans 12:2, NLT)

God's transformation in our lives begins with His transformation of our thoughts. The more we consider what God thinks about society, and our time on earth, the more we'll understand what He wants us to do.

### 6. Discuss how truth can be applied to everyday life.

> Wisdom...is not merely a matter of information or knowledge, but of skillful and practical application of the truth to the ordinary facets of life.[116]

Discuss different scenarios with your kids. Play the What If game: "What if...you're offered drugs, hit on by someone from the opposite sex, offered the answers to an upcoming quiz?" Talk through your children's responses with them.

Role-play with them what will happen when they do mess up. Let your children know they can come to you when they make bad choices: "What if...you watched a program that you know you shouldn't have, took something that wasn't yours, or hurt someone with your unkind words?" Model your loving response, your forgiveness, your willingness to pray with your child, and your willingness to stick it out. Everyone makes mistakes, and parents need to teach repentance and reconciliation as much as any other virtue.

The more you talk about "truth lived out," the more your kids will be able to face "anything goes" when the time comes. They will also be able to come to you when they slip, seeking your forgiveness and God's.

After all, isn't that what godly values are about?

## BONUS MATERIAL

### CLASHPOINT AROUND FEEDBACK:

***Traditionalists:*** "No news is good news."

***Baby Boomers:*** "Feedback once a year, with lots of documentation!"

***Generation Xers:*** "Sorry to interrupt, but how am I doing?"

***Millennials:*** "Feedback whenever I want it at the push of a button."[117]

# 18

# 1-2-3-4

## Counting on Education

***Step by step there's nothing to it....***

*Gloria Estefan & The Miami Sound Machine, Let It Loose, 1987, Epic*

I remember bringing home my report cards twice a year in yellow envelopes. As someone who did fairly well in school, I never faced the temptation of using a red ink pen to change a D to a B. I do remember my mom's response, though, as she glanced over the grades. "B-plus in history? It should have been an A." There were no attempts to help me with my homework, no rewards, no punishments, just one comment that told me I should do better.

Back when I was growing up, most of my classes had one teacher and a part-time aide. My mom didn't visit once a week to help out in class, but that was okay, because neither did any of the other moms. Parents showed up for the occasional field trip and Christmas concert. The other 99.9 percent of the time, education was between me and my educators.

I remember clearly the high school years of cutting class and forging my own permission form after the fact. I remember spending more time passing notes to friends than taking notes. And I remember not thinking twice about cheating on a test when I didn't have time to study...after all, a B-plus wasn't good enough. What I learned wasn't the most important thing; what showed up on the report card was.

I also remember being part of "new learning methods" when it came to education, such as doing breathing exercises and meditating in a darkened room as my science teacher played a recording of our vocabulary words. (Not that it helped. After flunking my first test, I realized even meditating couldn't take the place of actually studying.) I remember rock music played by the teacher in the classroom next door...it supposedly helped her students learn better. And the daily fluoride rinses that were as routine as the daily spelling quizzes. (I still got cavities. Go figure.) And looking back, realizing how much I didn't learn...it all makes me scratch my head over those "new ideals."

> As children, Xers didn't learn the alphabet in a measured singsong as did virtually everybody over fifty today. They shouted it out, one letter chasing another, as they learned to do on *Sesame Street*. They never slogged through grammar lessons of heartbreaking tedium. Instead, "Conjunction Junction" and the other upbeat lessons on *Schoolhouse Rock* were set to jazz riffs.[118]

Looking back, it didn't bother our parents that educators tried new and innovative ideas on us. What we learned was between us and the school.

That's not the case today.

Gen X parents are involved in education. For those of us who have children in school, we have access to our kids' attendance records, e-mail addresses for teachers, and in some school districts, parents can even check out what their children purchased for lunch. We want to know what's going on, because for the most part we faltered through the educational system on our own.

William Strauss, a leading author and researcher of generational differences, called parents who hovered and occasionally dropped into the system "helicopter parents." Of course, Gen Xers do nothing halfway, so instead of helicopters, we're considered "stealth fighter parents" who, Strauss claims, "move with stunning swiftness and know how to use technology when the need arises." He goes on to say:

> Boomer parents are more inclined to trust teachers and the education system. By contrast, Gen Xers will assume they have easy and direct access to teachers and expect *transparency* and *accountability* in everything from grades to safety.[119]

In fact, Gen Xers are the most involved parents the school system has ever seen, and their presence is being felt in all aspects of education—from preschool onward. We not only want our kids to learn the basics; we also want our children to be proficient in twenty-first century skills. After all, we don't worry that our children will keep up. Instead, we want them to lead the pack.

The Gen Xers are also driving the rush to charter and nontraditional schools, experts say, because they want schools to make their lives easier through direct marketing, practical solutions for their kids and individual attention.[120]

Does that sound like you?

## Individual Attention

I'll be the first to admit all the above statements are true about our family's view of education. At the age of three, my oldest son began attending preschool. It was only two days a week, and I spent one of those days in the classroom helping out. Fearful he wouldn't be able to keep up, I sacrificed my time and our checkbook to give Cory this opportunity. (And with my husband in college at the time, it *was* a sacrifice.)

But taking note of what happened in the preschool classroom, I soon realized I could do just as well as the teacher, and even provide more individualized learning through homeschooling. So when Cory hit kindergarten age, instead of enrolling him in a public or private school, I started teaching him at the kitchen table.

With his toddler sister running around and his baby brother on my lap, I spent two hours a day training him to read, write, add, and subtract. I also made biblical studies a core subject, placing as much focus on it as any other.

Learning became a natural part of our lives, and I enjoyed the time with my kids. Even now, I look back with fondness at the stories I read out loud, the Scripture verses recited in squeaky little voices, and the handmade skills chart lined with gold stars.

As the years went by the learning continued. Now, working at home with mom is the only educational system my children have known. Of course, there are activities we participate in outside of the home, such as sports teams, music lessons, and classes on foreign language and art, but even then, I know what's going on. I pick and choose, plot and plan.

In fact, Strauss's definition of our generation's desire for transparency and accountability in education is right on with me, too. I want to know what my kids have learned…in their minds *and* in their hearts. I also want to keep track of where they are, where they're going, and who they are with.

And while I take my role as teacher very seriously—working with my kids to reach their full academic potential—my main concern is the same as Paul's in his letter to Timothy:

> The purpose of my instruction is that all the Christians there would be filled with love that comes from a pure heart, a clear conscience, and sincere faith.
>
> (1 Timothy 1:5, NLT)

Of course, desiring the education of both the mind and the heart can be overwhelming at times. "Stealth fighter mode" is not an easy job. especially since my husband and I have claimed this additional task that most parents in the past didn't deal with.

To handle this role, whether it be as teacher or concerned parent, Gen Xers need to lead lives of transparency and accountability. Transparency to acknowledge the *why* behind our involvement, and accountability to admit that we are not our children's sole source for life and learning. As we step into the role of "educational director" for our kids, we realize we are also accountable to God for the decisions we make.

> And what kind of habitation pleases God? What must our natures be like before he can feel at home within us? He desires but sincerity, transparency, humility, and love. He will see to the rest.
>
> —A. W. Tozer, 1897–1963

## Straight from the Heart

***I've been dreamin', straight from the heart....***

**Bryan Adams, *Cuts Like a Knife*, 1983, A&M Records**

When I hear the word *transparency*, I think of something that can be seen through. It isn't something that can be seen in darkness. In fact, we only recognize something as transparent when a light is shined onto and filters through it.

We are foolish if we think there is any part of us hidden from God. Though we or the children we are raising may fool people on the outside, though we can educate our minds and stack up degrees and accreditations, God looks at our hearts.

The test of our transparency occurs only when God shines His light on us. And when it comes to the education of our children, only He can decipher our true values and motives. Why do we want our children to excel? Is it to see their names on the honor roll list? To ensure they get into the best colleges? As a bragging point to grandparents? Or can we truly say we desire for our children to reflect Christ in their education by doing their best, loving others, and walking in His ways?

While we want transparency in the educational system, God wants to view the motives behind our mission.

> Clearly, you are a letter from Christ prepared by us. It is written not with pen and ink, but with the Spirit of the living God. It is carved not on stone, but on human hearts. (2 Corinthians 3:3, NLT)

What is carved on your heart concerning your motives behind your children's education? If you're not sure, ask God to shine His light into your heart and tell you what He sees. You may be right on with your goals and dreams. Or there may be areas in which you're doing the right things, but with the wrong motives. You may even find educational concerns for your children that you've shrugged off. God wants to talk to you about those, too. No matter which of the above is true for you, God is faithful to shine His light on the situation.

## My Take On It

"Educational success is something that I want for my kids, but now I question my motives. Is it for me? For them? Where is God in all of this? I never really considered that He has a plan in whether my kids get straight As or not."

**—Shannon, Colorado**
**Born in 1971, mother of two**

# Is There Something I Should Know?

***Is there something I should say that would make you come my way....***

DURAN DURAN, ARENA, 1984, CAPITOL/EMI RECORDS

No matter what educational direction we choose for our children, as parents we are accountable to God first.

Author Elisabeth Elliot once said, "The fact that I am a woman does not make me a different kind of Christian, but the fact that I am a Christian does make me a different kind of woman."

The same is true for PTA parents: "The fact that I am a parent, concerned with my child's education, does not make me a different kind of Christian, but the fact that I am a Christian does make me a different kind of parent, concerned with my child's education."

Parents who seek Christ know that the end result of years of educational training should result in children who also seek Christ. In light of eternity, what could matter more?

> Teach me to do your will, for you are my God; may your good Spirit lead me on level ground. (Psalm 143:10)

God has a perfect plan for your children's future, and only He knows the best way to achieve it. It's not my job (or the job of any other writer or speaker) to inform you what path to choose concerning their education. But I guarantee if you seek God, He will clue you in on *His* desires. They might not be what you planned. But they will be perfect.

In fact, here are some questions to prayerfully consider:

- What is God speaking to my heart concerning my child's education?
- How does God's Word define success?

- What's best for my child?
- Will sending my child to a Christian school be too much of a financial burden on our family? Will public school require too much time or separation? What is required of homeschooling?
- What kind of environment does my child learn best in?
- What is God asking of me?

The good news is that God will not move you in a certain direction, and then leave you to flounder on your own.

God is available to guide our big decisions and our small ones, emotionally, spiritually, educationally…even to the end.

Maybe your children are still young and you're considering the numerous educational choices. God can help. Or maybe you're following the path you felt God leading you on, yet feel overwhelmed and ill-prepared for the task. God can help there, too. No matter what challenges you face, God is available with wisdom and support.

**For this God is our God forever and ever; he will be our guide even to the end.**
**(Psalm 48:14)**

But remember, the focus of His heart may be different from yours. You may envision an honor roll student, while God pictures a child with a humble and faithful heart. Don't let this world's opinion of educational success drown out God's still small voice.

Because in the end, God desires transparency and accountability from our children…not only during their school years, but for the rest of their lives.

## My Take On It

"Gen Xers want to provide their kids with the opportunities withheld from them [when they were kids]. There is huge social pressure to have our kids excelling at earlier and earlier ages. I'm appalled by how many preschool and daycare ads encourage parents to choose their services to 'nourish their future surgeon.' I suddenly feel concerned my children are not in Montessori preschools or other similarly challenging programs. Am I setting my kids up to fail in society? Why are we so competitive when it comes to our children and their future prospects?"

**—Heidi, Minnesota**
**Born in 1975, mother of two**

"I left a promising career to be a parent, yet I constantly worry that I am not doing a good job. Not only do I want to be home with my kids during their preschool years, but I also want to be home when they are in school. Our parents left us home alone, joining the workforce so that they could afford to send us to college. Yet for many of us, once we received a degree, we left the workforce to be home with our kids."

**—Jennifer R., Wisconsin**
**Born in 1969, mother of three**

## BONUS MATERIAL

Today, choices abound. Besides keeping up a house and yard, parents are chauffeuring vanloads of children to soccer, baseball, and dance class, dashing by the senior care facility to visit Grandma or Grandpa, running stepkids to and from the homes of both parents, and racing home to download the latest backlog of e-mails from work. And if the Palm Pilot shows a gap in the schedule, leisure choices abound. Rather than spending Sunday with a trip to church followed by Sunday dinner with the relatives, today's families have time and cash-consuming options like skiing, a trip to the cottage, or a spin on the boat. Aunts, uncles, and cousins who used to live down the block are now two thousand miles away. Attempts to bring whole families together involve more planning and cost almost as much as Desert Storm.[121]

# 19

# Be Good to Yourself

## Taking Care of Goals and Dreams

***Shoulder to shoulder, push and shove,***
***I'm hangin' up my boxin' gloves....***

**Journey, Raised on Radio, 1986, Columbia**

According to recent U.S. census data, 22 percent of moms with a graduate or professional degree are stay-at-home moms. What's more, in 6.4 percent of all marriages, the wife works and the husband is unemployed.[122] In fact, Gen Xers are the most educated moms in history.

The authors of *Mind the Gap* offer this perspective:

> The freedom Gen Xers want is to have balance in their lives. They want to be with their kids, to bathe them at night, watch them at ballet, play the drums, and kick a soccer ball with them at weekends. Few highly paid, demanding, 24/7 jobs are worth the price of not growing up with their families themselves. They are increasingly locating to out-of-town homes, whether in villages or the countryside, with their

computers, faxes, cell phones and the Internet, where they work long, hard hours but can opt to do so at night when the kids are asleep. The ability to do this is a great reward.[123]

While I have neither a graduate nor a professional degree, I am one of millions who attempt to simultaneously balance staying at home and working. (And yes, I live/work in a town of 20,000 in Montana with my computer, fax, and cell phone!)

From the moment I attended my first writers' conference, waddling from workshop to workshop (I was pregnant with my third baby), I knew without a doubt I would pour all my extra time, energy, and resources into being a published author. I fixed my eyes on a goal and moved toward it with enthusiasm. I wrote during my kids' nap times. I even set my alarm for 5 a.m. to have time to read my Bible, pray, and write before the kids awoke. And I learned three things as I focused on my goal:

**1. We can set a good example.** I have to admit, over the years there were moments I felt guilty for time set aside to work toward my dreams. When the kids got out of the toddler stage, every afternoon from 2 to 4 p.m., after our homeschooling day was done, I'd set aside "Mommy's writing time." It was easier to write when my kids still napped. They would sleep and I would write. But as they got older, they became jealous of the time I spent at the computer. "Play with us. We want to go to the park. Help me with this puzzle."

Of course, I had no reason to feel guilty. I had spent the entire morning with them, and I was available if they needed a snack, a drink, or to have their tushy wiped. Yet even as I helped my kids get situated with Legos or Play-Doh, a nagging voice in my head said, "A *good* mom would be over there with them, getting her hands sticky, in the middle of their play, interacting with them."

But another voice told me that God had given me this dream and this passion. I felt God's pleasure when I wrote. Which voice should I listen to?

I eventually discovered that my setting aside time "not focused" on my kids accomplished a few things:

1 They learned how to entertain themselves. Unlike some of their friends, they didn't need mom around to orchestrate their play.

2 Cory, Leslie, and Nathan knew what it meant for me to set a goal and strive to accomplish it. They saw me work, then they witnessed the efforts as my articles, and eventually books, began showing up in the mail.

3 As an added bonus, my two older kids are now working on books of their own. If Mom can sit in her pajamas and pound out words that people want to buy, why can't they?

**2. Sometimes God's dreams are different from ours.** Despite the peace I experienced with my writing, I wasn't always right-on about where my dreams were taking me. For years I had my heart set on seeing my name in print...but God had a different plan. In fact, as I attempted to balance my time juggling writing and my family, God added a few more balls to my act. These included founding a Crisis Pregnancy Center in my community and working with teen moms.

I prayed, *But, Lord, I can't do those things. I won't have time to write. What about all the people who will be reached with my words?*

His response: *And what about all the people in your community I wish to reach with My light?*

Ouch.

So, while I continued to write occasionally, I obediently headed in this new direction. And as I worked to fulfill God's vision for our community, I discovered that my kids enjoyed being part of the vision.

At the new center, they folded donated baby clothes. When a beautiful Victorian home was donated to our growing ministry, my kids and husband helped rip up old carpet, add a new layer of paint, solicit donations, and babysit for the teenage mothers who attended support meetings.

Which leads to the third thing I learned...

**3. Sometimes as we follow our goals and dreams, God shapes our children's hearts.** As I worked to serve God in this new capacity, my kids invariably discovered the world didn't center around them. (What a concept!)

They saw that God had called their mom and dad to give and serve in His kingdom, and that many people in our community (and the world) needed to know God's love.

It's amazing how easy it is for me to develop a list of goals that *I* want to accomplish. I picked one thing—writing—that I felt "called to." But God showed me how limited my vision was. Jerry Bridges puts it this way in *The Practice of Godliness*:

> Whether we have several gifts or only one, whether our gifts put us in a position of prominence or keep us always behind the scenes, the important truth is that those gifts have been given to us by grace. We did not deserve them; we did not earn them; they were sovereignly bestowed upon us. I don't deserve to be where I am in the body of Christ, and the prominent person doesn't deserve to be where he is. We are each in our place by God's grace.[124]

What I accomplished, along with everything yet to be done, is only possible because of God's grace bestowed upon me. God showed me how *He* was able to intertwine my dreams with the character development I desired for my own children. Talk about abundant grace!

When I think back and consider my prayers, I realize God gave me a two-for-one. I walked in God's callings, and my heart's desires were met as I prayed for my children to have:

- hearts to serve God
- the desire to share Jesus' love
- faithfulness
- compassion
- consideration for others
- purpose

God was not only working with me during those years to fulfill the desires He placed on my heart; He was also teaching my kids to become the people He desires them to be.

## My Take On It

"The concept of balancing motherhood and following my own God-given goals and dreams has always been a real struggle for me. I've always wanted to be a mother, but at the same time I never had the vision some of my friends and sister had of having children and staying home. I've always wanted more.I live in a happy compromise. Most weeks I'm an attorney three days a week, and home the rest of the week. This is an option I am incredibly blessed to have."

**—Cara, Indiana**
**Born in 1974, mother of two**

"I was thinking about what it was like for boomers—both their struggles and the things they had easy. One thing that makes it so difficult for mothers of small children is that we hardly get a break. When I was six, my parents would send me out the back door and I would roam the neighborhood for an hour or more, riding my bike, climbing trees. In suburbia, we have a tiny backyard and my kids grow bored within three minutes. We can't send them out front for fear they'll be kidnapped. So we're stuck entertaining them, or praying they'll find something to entertain themselves."

**—Rene, Oklahoma**
**Born in 1972, mother of two**

## Purposeful

Through the years of seeking my goals and dreams—for myself, my career, and my family—I've discovered one more thing. God wants us to be obedient to the purposes He has for us, no matter what stage of life we're in…even the parenting stage.

> It is difficult to state what your purpose in life is, because God has moved you into His purpose through the Holy Spirit. He is using you now for His purposes throughout the world as He used His Son for the purpose of our salvation. If you seek great things for yourself, thinking, "God has called me for this and for that," you barricade God from using you.
>
> I must learn that the purpose of my life belongs to God, not me. God is using me from His great personal perspective, and all He asks of me is that I trust Him…. When I stop telling God what I want, he can freely work His will in me without any hindrance.[125]

Actress Bette Davis once wrote:

> To fulfill a dream,
> To be allowed to sweat over lonely labor,
> To be given a chance to create,
> Is the meat and potatoes of life.
> The money is gravy.[126]

The question is, *Whose dream are you sweating over? Yours or God's?* The former will leave you spinning your wheels frustrated. The latter will lead to "immeasurably more than all we ask or imagine" (Ephesians 3:20). The choice seems clear to me. Clear, of course, but not always easy to follow.

So, how can we know we're on the right track? What dreams should we follow? And how can we insure they are the ones that will take both us and our children on God's chosen path? Here are a few verses to clue us in:

> For I have come down from heaven to do the will of God who sent me, not to do what I want. (John 6:38, NLT)

> And I am sure that God, who began the good work within you, will continue his work until it is finally finished on that day when Christ Jesus comes back again. (Philippians 1:6, NLT)

> Don't act thoughtlessly, but try to understand what the Lord wants you to do...let the Holy Spirit fill and control you. (Ephesians 5:17–18, NLT)

> God's secret plan has now been revealed to us; it is a plan centered on Christ, designed long ago according to his good pleasure. (Ephesians 1:9, NLT)

By reading these verses, I'm able to narrow my focus to five things *God* sees as most important:

1. Just like Jesus, our role here on earth is to do what God wants, not what we think up.
2. When God begins a good work in us, He is faithful to complete it.
3. We need to think before we act. It's obvious, I know, but it's ironic that people tend to put more effort into planning a two-week vacation than thinking about the destiny of their earthly journey. (I'm guilty of this, too.) Yet Got desires that we seek His will to discover His plan for our lives.
4. Once we understand what the Lord wants, we need to let the Holy Spirit fill us and control us. God usually has big plans for us. Bigger

than anything we could think up. Bigger than anything we could accomplish in our own strength. (But remember, big to God may not be big to us.)

> A single day in your courts is better than a thousand anywhere else! I would rather be a gatekeeper in the house of my God than live the good life in the homes of the wicked. (Psalm 84:10, NLT)

**5** The plan God has for us is centered on Christ. This is what brings Him good pleasure.

As children of God who are "fearfully and wonderfully made," God has granted us unique gifts for the benefit of His kingdom. There is no better way for our children to learn about *their* gifts than by seeing us fulfill *ours*... through the grace and strength found in God alone.

So don't be afraid to seek God concerning His dreams...not only for yourself as a mother, but also as a child of the Most High. Trust that His dreams for you are "immeasurably more than all we ask or imagine"!

# BONUS MATERIAL

## WHAT DOES THE FUTURE HOLD FOR OUR KIDS?

### Statement 1:

Today's kids are on track to become a powerhouse generation, full of technology planners, community shapers, institution builders, and world leaders, perhaps destined to dominate the twenty-first century like today's fading and ennobled G.I. Generation dominated the twentieth. Millennials have a solid chance to become America's next great generation.[127]

### Statement 2:

Today's Millennial children should bask in adult hope, remain upbeat themselves, and reject the Unraveling-era cynicism that surrounds them. They should keep their innocence and avoid growing up too quickly. They should do small deeds while dreaming of the day they will do greater ones. By applying peer pressure to positive purposes, they will be able to reconstruct a positive reputation for American adolescence. When older generations preach traditional values that they themselves failed to learn as children (and which are not yet common in the adult world), Millennials would do well to ignore the hypocrisy—and heed the lessons....

At the onset of the Great Depression, President Herbert Hoover demanded "a fair chance" for American youth: "If we could have but one generation of properly born, trained, educated and healthy children, a thousand other problems of government would vanish." Events—and young G.I.s—proved him right. The Millennials' time is near. If they play their script well, perhaps the day will come when they sing in unison, as young patriots did in 1776. "The rising world shall sing of us a thousand years to come / And tell our children's children the wonders we have done.[128]

## Statement 3:

If my people, who are called by my name, will humble themselves and pray and seek my face and turn from their wicked ways, then will I hear from heaven and will forgive their sin and will heal their land. (2 Chronicles 7:14)

**And just imagine...God chose us to raise this amazing generation of kids!**

# 20 Danger Zone

## Organized Activities: How Much Is Too Much?

***Revvin' up your engine....***

*Kenny Loggins, Top Gun soundtrack, 1986, Sony Records*

My five-year-old daughter twirled onstage in her pink tutu. It was her dance recital, and even though I'd driven her forty-five minutes twice a week to dance lessons, she was forgetting at least half the dance steps. Where was the tiny prima ballerina I envisioned when I signed her up?

The fact was, my daughter was more thrilled with her sequined costume than the dance routine. And she was more excited about the cookies served afterward than the recital itself.

But I didn't learn my lesson from that experience. Believing T ball to be a must for every boy, I signed Cory up. He hated the sport and spent more time writing his name in the dirt with the toe of his cleat than watching the ball.

Soccer, basketball, and art lessons followed—each new activity propelled by my understanding of what constitutes an idyllic childhood. My desire to see my kids excel fueled the sacrifice of numerous practices and weekends spent at the ball field. And with each new event, I ignored the complaints echoing from the backseat of my minivan: "But Mom, do I have to?"

"Of course you have to. You'll like it," I responded, pressing the gas pedal a little harder so we wouldn't be late.

*I never got to* ______________________.
*Some of my best memories were* ________________________.
*What will all the other parents think if we don't* ______________________?

My thoughts weren't centered solely around creating idyllic childhoods for my children; also at stake was my reputation as a mother. *Other parents sign their kids up for sports* and *art,* I reasoned. *Not to mention music* and *foreign language lessons.*

If I cared—*truly* cared—I'd give my kids the best, right?

One day I was reading my Bible when I innocently came across this verse:

> You insult your Maker when you exploit the powerless; when you're kind to the poor, you honor God. (Proverbs 14:31, *The Message*)

*Read that again,* I felt God telling me. *Isn't that what you're doing to your kids?*

My kids?

I read the verse again. Was God telling me they were the powerless ones and I was exploiting them? Surely He was talking about the "poor" poor—you know, the homeless guy who stands at the intersection by Wal-Mart holding a sign?

I read the verse a dozen times, and images of my little ballerina, my soccer players, and my T-ball shortstop came to mind. Was I really insulting God by forcing my kids to participate in all these activities they had no desire to be part of?

I decided to check it out. I discovered the word *poor* here is translated as "in the sense of want, destitute, needy."[129] In other places, it means "the least of these."

Who could be more in need of us than our children? Who could be more powerless than those whom we exhibit our power over on a daily basis?

Not that we, as parents, set out to be cruel. Actually, in our hearts we truly want our children to have the best of everything. The problem arises when what we think is "best" for our children is different from what their Maker designed.

My two oldest children love books and movies, drama, giving speeches, and music. Looking back, I can clearly see how many years I wasted trying to make them participate in the activities "all the other kids" were doing.

My youngest son makes up creative stories, and then he and his friends act out these adventures with their Beanie Babies. How sad it makes me now to think of those countless hours Nathan spent mindlessly maneuvering around the basketball court, following the coach's orders. *I* forced him to sign up—"for socialization and exercise," I told myself. I realize now he could have received both by running around the front yard with his friends, leading them on fanciful adventures.

> Oh yes, you shaped me first inside, then out; you formed me in my mother's womb. I thank you, High God—you're breathtaking! Body and soul, I am marvelously made! I worship in adoration—what a creation! You know me inside and out, you know every bone in my body; You know exactly how I was made, bit by bit, how I was sculpted from nothing into something. Like an open book, you watched me grow from conception to birth; all the stages of my life were spread out before you, the days of my life all prepared before I'd even lived one day. (Psalm 139:13–16, *The Message*)

In forming our children, God did not create empty vessels, making it the parents' job to fill them, to form their personalities, and to insert creativity or skill into their brains. Rather, God designed our children and turned them over to us to mold into the shape He's already crafted. How silly to think the same sports, or art lessons, or music lessons, or anything else the world prescribes will be just the things my children need. Who wants "well-rounded" if God has crafted a unique and special shape?

Timothy Jones, author of *Nurturing a Child's Soul*, says:

> Only as we take time to understand our children *as they are* will we truly welcome them as God's handiwork. Only as we realize that they come into the world as unique beings, with differing gifts and temperaments and needs, can we rightly nurture them. We learn to observe who they are, respecting them as unique, irrepeatable creations.
>
> Making room for a child also means letting go of some of our perfectionism, some of our unrealistic expectations, our insensitive, too-high expectations.[130]

As I thought about this, God brought to mind other events—like the drama class my oldest son and daughter recently signed up for. They come home excited after every class, praising their "so funny" teacher, describing what they learned and the activities they participated in. That class is a perfect fit for their God-given personalities.

Isn't that what it's all about—becoming students of our children and discovering their unique shapes?

## My Take On It

"Why would I think that God wouldn't provide opportunities for my children to develop the gifts He gave them? Why do I think that it is all up to me?"

**—Jennifer R., Wisconsin**
**Born in 1969, mother of three**

"I have found my kids are usually stressed out about being late, or they really don't want to attend the event at all. (They just have to because we have added it to their list of 'good things to do.') Many parents do put their kids in everything. This leaves the parents as glorified taxi drivers with no time for parenting. I worry that our kids are missing out on the 'meat and potatoes' of a solid home life."

**—Lisa P., Nevada**
**Born in 1969, mother of three**

# Under Pressure

***What this world is about....***

*Queen, Live Magic, 1986, Hollywood*

So what's a parent to do? Should we stop everything cold turkey and hope for the best? Actually, as Christian parents who desire to raise up a new generation of believers, our single most important commitment should be to God. Any successes will flow from that commitment.

What does this commitment entail when it comes to parenting? That will differ for each family. Here are some Scripture verses to help keep us all on track:

Do not conform any longer to the pattern of this world, but be transformed by the renewing of your mind. Then you will be able to test and approve what God's will is—his good, pleasing and perfect will. (Romans 12:2)

We are all parts of his one body, and each of us has different work to do. And since we are all one body in Christ, we belong to each other, and each of us needs all the others. God has given each of us the ability to do things well. (Romans 12:5-6, NLT)

LORD, you establish peace for us; all that we have accomplished you have done for us. (Isaiah 26:12)

From these verses, here are some questions you can ask yourself concerning which activities to choose for your children:

1. Why am I signing my child up for this activity? Am I doing it so my child won't be left out? Am I "conforming to the pattern of this world"?
2. Have I asked God about His thoughts? Have I renewed my mind? (It seems silly, I know, to seek God about whether or not to sign a child up for soccer. Yet isn't that what "lordship" is all about—making God Lord over all areas of our lives?)
3. Does this activity fit in with my child's natural talents and gifts? Has God given my child the ability to do this activity well? Will this activity benefit the body of Christ?
4. Does the activity accomplish peace in our household? Can you see God at work?

I'll be the first to admit that cutting back isn't easy. But don't think of it that way. Rather than eliminating, think of this as *refocusing*—on God, on your child's God-given abilities and gifts, and on God's plans for *His* kingdom. When you cut away at the world's idea of a "perfect" childhood, God will be sure to show you what He considers *perfect* for your child!

Isn't that the best focus of all?

## My Take On It

"Often I have felt the Lord telling me I need to slow down. To spend quality time with my children. It made me feel terrible when I looked at the way I'd been parenting. But I gave that guilt to God. He took it away, and I went on my parenting journey with the best advice from God Himself."

**—Abbey, South Dakota**
**Born in 1977, mother of two**

"I have been overwhelmed by all the activities children are involved in after school and during the summer. It has been a struggle deciding what is best for my kids. But at ages ten, six, and three, I feel they need me (and their daddy) more than anyone or anything else in this world. The world will get them soon enough."

**—Kristy, Texas**
**Born in 1971, mother of three**

## BONUS MATERIAL

Teenagers often embrace the current social issues, believing their opinions to be more enlightened and superior to their parents' archaic views on life. Teenagers in the '60s tried to be more racially tolerant than their parents. Teens of the '80s were more in touch with the ecological needs of our planet. Teens of the '90s have been more politically correct and therefore much more tolerant of those who are different from themselves.[131]

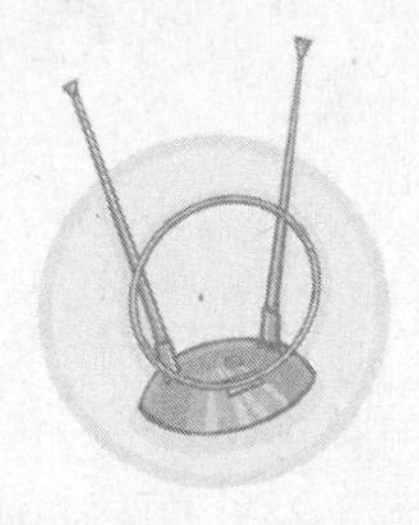

# 21 In My Dreams

## To Compare or Not Compare

***Running in circles, waiting to see you in my dreams....***

**DOKKEN, *UNDER LOCK AND KEY*, 1985, ELEKTRA ENTERTAINMENT**

A few years ago a new guy started working at my husband's office. Skyler seemed like a nice guy, and my husband asked if we could invite his family over for dinner.

"I hear his wife Tara is nice," John told me. "I think you'd like her."

I would gladly have invited them over—except that Tara's reputation had preceded her. You see, my idea of dinner with guests starts with frozen lasagna, bagged salad, and store-bought garlic bread. Tara, on the other hand, was purported to prepare all manner of culinary delights for her guests—and top the meal off with homemade dessert. Rumor had it that Tara's shelves were lined with jars of produce she grew and canned herself, and that she also made her own quilts and hand-stamped her own greeting cards. I was intimidated, to say the least.

The first time we met, at an office Christmas party, Tara was polite but reserved—and I was no better. I found out later that Tara was just as intimidated by what she had heard about *me*, the published author, homeschooling mother, and children's church director. In fact, as certain as I was that I fell far below Tara's standards, she was just as certain that she could never live up to mine.

Then one morning I felt God leading me to invite Tara and her family over for dinner. I asked my husband to make the arrangements and set to work on my best recipe—chicken enchiladas. When Tara called to accept our dinner invitation, she insisted on bringing dessert, confessing that she had over a dozen homemade pies stored in her freezer. How could I say no?

Dinner turned out great, but it was the conversation afterward that proved the turning point in our friendship. While Tara and I were strolling through the woods behind my house, she asked me about church. I shared about my family's relationship with the Lord, and her face glowed with excitement.

Before the evening was over, Tara and her husband had made plans to join us at a Bible study the following week. Soon they began regularly attending worship services, and a few months later both were baptized.

Once Tara and I became friends, the truth about our initial qualms came out. We discovered that we had both been so busy agonizing over our own shortcomings that we had successfully avoided each other for more than a year.

I'm happy to report that Tara is now one of my closest friends. But I shudder to think how my own insecurities almost kept us from getting to know each other.

So what gives? Why are we as parents often so concerned with how we compare to others that we miss out on enjoying friends, family, and life in general?

## My Take On It

"Are Xers more motivated by guilt than other generations? I see so many of my friends struggling with guilt and not just in the area of parenting. It seems to be a primary motivator in all areas of an Xer's life, and Boomer parents seem to have tapped into this guilt motivator. My Xer friends often have divorced, self-consumed boomer parents that basically emotionally abandoned them, and yet it's my Xer friends that feel guilty. God's grace is the answer to guilt, but how do Xers make that 'real'?"

**—Jennifer R., Wisconsin**
**Born in 1969, mother of three**

"I don't think Gen Xers are very honest with each other. We have this vision of Supermom in our heads. We are supposed to be able to clothe, feed, care for, and nurture our kids and our marriage and our careers while saying yes to every request for help at school, church, and social clubs. We cart our kids all over the place so they don't miss any vital opportunities. We take no time for ourselves, and we tell the world that we are doing great. Why do Gen X parents think they have to go it alone or that they are the only ones struggling? Is it pride? It's as though we say, 'Everyone else looks like they are handling it just fine, why can't I?'"

**—Heidi, Minnesota**
**Born in 1975, mother of two**

"We may crave the accolades of others or lose focus because of what others think, but we should keep our eyes on the prize: pleasing God. To hear, 'Well done, good and faithful servant' at the end of our life—that, truly, is all that really matters."

**—Judy, New York**
**Born in 1965, mother of two**

## Unscripted

So what do we do now? Xers realize we have a problem with comparing ourselves, but where do we turn?

### 1. Discover your passion...and be okay with it.

> Looking for renewal in our lives, sometimes we miss the obvious: where our real passion and love lie. Grace is present there. How easy it is to follow other people's scripts, busying ourselves with books and seminars detailing how we should become fulfilled and renewed—and all the while ignore what really energizes us. Why are we so afraid of following our deepest passion? Perhaps we fear failing.... Hope allows us to accept the risk of committing all our energies to what gives us life, confident that wherever it leads us will be worth the effort.[132]

Through my experience with Tara, I realized it was okay that we both followed different passions. I focused my energies on rearing kids, writing books, and ministering in church, while she found her joy in cooking, canning, crafting, and...rearing kids. I was comparing my weaknesses with her strengths instead of realizing we each excelled in different areas.

> **Be sure to do what you should, for then you will enjoy the personal satisfaction of having done your work well, and you won't need to compare yourself to anyone else. For we are each responsible for our own conduct.**
>
> (Galatians 6:4–5, NLT)

Just as each of our kids is special and unique, we need to accept that the same is true of us as parents, too. We won't do everything well, and we shouldn't expect ourselves to.

As long as I can stand before my Maker and see pleasure in His eyes, I don't need to wonder about what others think...or worry I don't measure up.

When I seek God, do what He asks, find joy where my passion lies, and feel His pleasure, then comparisons cease to matter.

2. Cultivate a quiet heart. Bombarding images of "ideal" parents on television sitcoms and in print media can make anyone feel inferior. Instead of being content with who we are, we often make mental lists of what we are not. Rather than be content with what God has given us, we chide ourselves for not doing more and being more.

> God, I'm not trying to rule the roost, I don't want to be king of the mountain. I haven't meddled where I have no business or fantasized grandiose plans. I've kept my feet on the ground, I've cultivated a quiet heart. Like a baby content in its mother's arms, my soul is a baby content. (Psalm 131:1–2, *The Message*)

Remember the peaceful smile on your baby's face as you rocked him in your arms? How he fell asleep listening to your heartbeat? In the same way, God's arms are open and He wants nothing more than for us to find contentment there. We don't need to be king of the mountain, queen of the slim and beautiful, prince of the popular, or princess of grandiose plans. Through prayer and focus on God, our quiet hearts will remind us *He* is enough.

3. Conform to Christ. Neil Anderson and Robert Saucy, authors of *The Common Made Holy*, write:

> Conforming to the image of God is a long and steady process of internal change as we abide in Christ. People simply do not change overnight, nor can they be forced to do so. Abiding in Christ is being yoked to the gentle Jesus (Matthew 11:29).[133]

When we are focused on Jesus, the people around us grow peripheral. We may still see things we need to change in order to become more like Jesus, but they will be things we aren't expected to accomplish in our own strength. When Jesus points out areas we are lacking, He will also be faithful to guide us and empower us as we join Him.

## My Take On It

"Okay, I want to be the perfect stay-at-home mom who homeschools and bakes cookies. But is that reality? I can be that best mom by showing and telling my kids that I love them and appreciate them every day."

**—Brenda, Minnesota**
**Born in 1967, mother of four**

"Some of the biggest challenges in raising kids in today's society come from peer pressure. Not just the peer pressure that kids will face in school, but the pressure from other parents. There's the group who think you should sign your children up for everything. There's the group that compares their children's abilities to everyone else's. There's the group that goes 'all natural'—no candy, pop, junk food, TV, or any other 'rotting' influences. We go through life feeling like we are the only ones who ignore the pile of dishes on the counter and long for the quiet time of a child's favorite TV show. What's hard to learn is that we are not alone."

**—Jennifer H., Minnesota**
**Born in 1974, mother of two**

"I think we fear rejection. Many of our generation were rejected by their parents. We've all been rejected by peers at some point. So we build walls and do it all in an attempt to avoid more hurt that is inflicted when we fail to be all we are expected to be. Inside we die from the pressure. But we don't know how to get off the rollercoaster of fear and isolation."

**—Cara, Indiana**
**Born in 1974, mother of two**

"Yes, I feel inadequate! Yes, I think I have to do everything on my own. When did 'help' become a dirty word? This is definitely an area where I struggle. Control freak? Who, me? Okay, maybe just a little."

**—Michelle D., New Jersey**
**Born in 1968, mother of one**

*

## The Other Side of Life

***Baby, baby, baby, let's investigate....***

*The Moody Blues, The Other Side of Life, 1986, Polygram Records, Inc.*

Of course, it's not just ourselves and our parenting skills that we compare, but our children, too. Right from the beginning, I labeled my kids certain ways: He's a handful. She's shy. Why can't he be calm like the neighbor's kid? Why can't she be more outgoing like the other kids in Sunday school?

I then repeated these labels that I placed on my children to others—often in front of my kids. And, of course, they continued to act that way. It was as if my words were placing curses upon the heads of my kids.

Later, after I realized what I was doing, I silenced my thoughts and shut my mouth. And I discovered that my kids weren't like that at all. Yes, my son was active, but he was also very intelligent and kind. And my daughter wasn't shy; we just hadn't given her the proper tools for carrying on a conversation. Once John and I worked with Leslie, she did great—in fact, today *no one* would accuse that outgoing bundle of energy of being shy.

Yet comparing my kids to others was only one of my mistakes. Another was that I labeled my kids and then wondered why they didn't behave differently.

Naturally, this smacks of negative labels. What about all the positive ones—where are they? What difference would it make if we, as a group of parents, started looking at our kids as a generation where hope can abound?

Look at what the authors of *Millennials Rising* have to say about the next generation's potential:

> Boomers and Gen Xers realize that neither of their generations is likely to be remembered as a generation of heroes. Perhaps, however, both can someday be remembered as the leaders, educators, and parents who shaped a generation of heroes.[134]

I like that!

Eighteen years ago, when I was my oldest son's age, I spent evenings watching horror films and weekends drinking with friends. I was already sexually active, and I spent more time keeping track of my lies than speaking truth.

In comparison, although my son's not perfect, he hangs out with good kids, enjoys swing dancing and bowling, and has made a commitment to remain pure in all areas of his life. He enjoys basketball and volunteers time helping his youth pastor. He enjoys hanging out at home with dear old mom and dad. He comes to us when he messes up or needs advice. Most of all, he loves God.

If there is any comparing going on, it should not concern how we're measuring ourselves against other parents or how our children are measuring up to other kids. Rather, with God's grace, we should be concerned with how our generation raises the next one to serve God and care for others.

> Train a child in the way he should go, and when he is old he will not turn from it. (Proverbs 22:6)

This is what the *Nelson Study Bible* says about Proverbs 22:6.

> The verb for *train* means "to dedicate," and the word for *way* generally refers to living correctly in God's sight. Solomon was advising parents to set their child aside for special use, to dedicate him or her to the Lord and His path. The verb train includes the idea of stimulating the child to do good—through words of guidance, discipline, and encouragement on the right path. This is a parent's main task, to receive a child as a charge from the Lord and then to dedicate the child to God's ways.[135]

After all, isn't that what we're doing...dedicating the next generation to God's ways? There's no comparison. It's exactly where God wants us—and exactly what our children need most.

# BONUS MATERIAL

## ATTITUDE ABOUT GOD

***GIs:*** God is distant and aloof.

***Silents:*** God is distant but approachable.

***Boomers:*** God is familiar—we can feel His power working through us.

***Xers:*** God is a friend, guide, companion, and healer.

***Millennials:*** God is the nation builder, provider, and protector.[136]

# 22 KEEPING the Faith

## Fired-Up Family Devotions

***Still I would not be here now, if I never had the hunger....***

BILLY JOEL, AN INNOCENT MAN, 1983, COLUMBIA

The Bible is filled with uplifting stories, odd occurrences, and passages which hurt my heart. One that saddens me most is found in Judges 2:8–12.

> Then Joshua son of Nun, the servant of the LORD, died at the age of 110.... After that generation died, another generation grew up who did not acknowledge the LORD or remember the mighty things he had done for Israel. Then the Israelites did what was evil in the LORD's sight and worshiped the images of Baal. They abandoned the LORD, the God of their ancestors, who had brought them out of Egypt. (NLT)

Can you imagine? The men and women who entered the Promised Land, who circled the walls of Jericho, who saw God's hand in defeating the giants in the land, *did not* pass on the knowledge of God to their children.

No one knows why these things weren't passed on. Maybe they were busy building homes or tending fields in this new land. For whatever reason, they did not acknowledge God…and as a result, their children did not *know Him.* It was the very thing their great leader, Moses, had warned about:

> "Only be careful, and watch yourselves closely so that you do not forget the thing your eyes have seen or let them slip from your heart as long as you live. Teach them to your children and to their children after them." (Deuteronomy 4:9)

When it comes to training our children to be devoted to God, it's not about blazing a trail and hoping they follow. It's not about living on God's promises and expecting them to catch on. It's about firing up our kids' hearts toward seeking and serving God. It's about empowering them to approach God on their own. We can do this by training through Bible study, worship, and prayer.

Here is what the authors of *Mind the Gap* write on this subject:

> The Xers' childhood experiences of broken relationships (divorce) has resulted in small group experiences being attractive to them, especially when there is an emphasis on family and relationships. For them, faith is best expressed in a small community where the reality of the daily outworking of faith can be expressed so they can see faith translating into action.[137]

As Gen Xers, we like the idea of small group experiences. And what better small group can you imagine than your own family? It is among this small group of people that God desires to work, allowing each family member to see faith put into action. It is here, as we teach our children the things of God, that the idea of approaching the Creator of our universe becomes real and possible.

# Urgent

***Emer...emer...emer... It's urgent!***

FOREIGNER, RECORDS, 1982, ATLANTIC

I don't need to spend much time within these pages relating the importance of family devotions. We all know it's important. The question is, then, why don't we do it? One main reason is often our unspoken fears.

**1. Fear of inadequacy.** One reason we don't take time to teach our kids is we fear we don't know the Bible ourselves. The good news is God doesn't depend on us to know it all. He simply wants us to be a vessel He can use. Here's a great story from Tony Evans' *The Fire That Ignites* that illustrates that point:

> When I was a boy growing up in Baltimore, the fire marshal would sometimes come around on a hot summer afternoon and flush out one of the fire hydrants. Water would surge up out of the hydrant and come splashing down on the street, and all of us kids would put on short pants and run through it. That was our inner-city swimming pool.
>
> But it posed a problem in my mind. I couldn't figure out how that three-foot-high hydrant could produce so much water, hour after hour.
>
> I decided to ask my dad: "Dad, how can that little pipe hold all that water?"
>
> He smiled and said, "Son, that pipe is empty." Then he explained that the hydrant was joined underground with other pipes that were connected to a reservoir—a lake that held more water than I could imagine, more than we could all use even on the hottest summer afternoon. The rush of water from the hydrant was made possible by that hidden connection to a boundless, unseen source of water.
>
> We're like that empty hydrant pipe; we hold nothing in ourselves,

> but the Holy Spirit is our invisible connection to almighty God, who has an infinite reservoir of refreshment that never runs dry. Because of that connection, you can open up your life to Him at any time and experience the living waters flowing up from your innermost being, meeting your every need.[138]

I love that! We don't have to be worried about having "enough inside us" to lead our children. Throughout our entire lives there will always be something more to learn about God and His kingdom. Instead, we need to be an open valve for God to flow through. He does not call us to train up our children, and then leave us stranded. Rather, He asks us to open ourselves so He can flow through.

**2. Fear of time commitment.** This is a biggie for most families. We have enough going on—do we really want to add another thing to our busy lives? The good news is publishers are coming out with more family-friendly materials all the time. There are devotional materials available for our car rides, dinnertime, and even TV time.

Also, whether we use prepackaged materials or do our own thing, we shouldn't feel as if we have to host a mini-church service. It's better to do something, anything, even if it's just reading one Scripture verse over dinner and talking about it.

**3. Fear of rejection.** I think this is my biggest fear as a parent. What if my kids think I'm lame or my spouse doesn't want to participate?

I'm not going to fool myself into thinking this book is going to be accepted by moms and dads alike. I know many of my readers will be women. And out of all you moms, quite a few will deal with the issue of having a husband who isn't on board when it comes to family devotions.

If that's the case, here are some tips from Lou Priolo, author of *Teach Them Diligently: How to Use the Scriptures in Child Training*:

- Keep in mind that since each family is unique and there is no "right" way to have family devotions, the frequency and structure will be different for every family.

- Use mealtime as a natural time to have "family time." (Many households find the time immediately following the evening meal to be best suited for family time.)

- Be creative. Variety is the spice of life when it comes to Bible study and "family time."

- Consider the ages of the children. Families with several young children will find it more difficult to establish a "family time." Don't be discouraged. Kids grow up! Additionally, fathers are more likely to be involved with structured Bible times with their child as they mature.

- Be flexible. Don't be legalistic. Allow for changes in the family, schedule, or needs of the children.

Priolo also offers this advice for frustrated moms:

Be careful not to get so discouraged with your husband's mishandling of family devotions that it becomes a source of bitterness in your own heart and a point of contention in your marriage. Don't elevate your own desire for your husband to initiate family devotions above the commands of Scripture. Don't turn this good desire into an idolatrous one! A man's commitment to lead "formal family devotions" is not necessarily a barometer of his spiritual maturity or his desire to lead the family spiritually. Guard your heart against comparing your husband or your family to anyone else. An older woman I know once said, "I count it a blessing to have a husband who lived devotionally rather than having one who only led devotions."[139]

## My Take On It

"I hear preachers tell me that the parents are the kids' first glimpse of God, and then I start feeling sorry for my kids, because they're getting a lousy glimpse!"

**—Rene, Oklahoma**
**Born in 1972, mother of two**

"I tell my children that when we don't know an answer, we ask God for wisdom. I have verses taped up all over my house; no matter where we go, there is the Word of God."

**—Tiffany, Michigan**
**Born in 1976, mother of four**

"Passing the torch is a burden of my heart. I want to instill a love for God into my two boys. I want faith to become theirs. Just last night my oldest boy asked me to get him up early, so he could have time to shower and do a devotion before school. Wow!"

**—Scott, Washington**
**Born in 1968, father of two**

"My parents did not receive Christ until I was a married adult. Growing up I really had no connection to Christ, or anything He accomplished for us. We became Christians before starting our family, and I pray that we would begin a legacy. Our family is different because our morals and values are Bible-based, unchanging."

**—Tonia, Idaho**
**Born in 1970, mother of two**

# Top Three Focuses for Fired-Up Devotions:

**1. Read God's Word...and remind your children these are the very words of God.** The God who created the universe, who spoke galaxies into existence—He is the One who gave us *these* very words we are reading.

"Christ's words have permanent value because of His person," says W. H. Griffith Thomas. "They endure because He endures."

We read in Matthew 24:35, "Heaven and earth will pass away, but [Christ's] words will never pass away."

**2. Praise God...with a joyful heart.** "God's purpose was that we who were the first to trust in Christ should praise our glorious God" (Ephesians 1:12, NLT).

Some of my best memories are of lining up my preschoolers on miniature plastic chairs and having "praise time" before my husband went off to work. We either sang our favorite Sunday School songs or put in a Bible songs cassette to sing along with.

Even today, a smile fills my face when I hear my kids singing praise songs in the car or while they're busy working around the house. Music has a way of embedding in our hearts and minds until we can't help but release it.

**3. Prayer...changes hearts.** One of my favorite stories concerning prayer time happened when my three kids were staying over at my friend Twyla's house. When it was time for all five kids to say their bedtime prayers, Twyla told them, "Tonight we're going to do 'popcorn prayers.' Everyone pray one sentence, starting from the youngest and moving to the oldest."

Everyone closed their eyes and waited for my son, Nathan—the youngest—to begin. When he didn't begin praying after twenty seconds, Twyla opened her eyes. That's when she realized Nathan had his hand raised. "Uh, Mrs. Klundt?" he said politely. "I forgot the rules."

The best thing about prayer is there are no rules! Simply remind your kids that prayer involves us sharing our hearts with God—and keeping ourselves open for God to share His heart with us.

Finally, remember family devotions should not be our sole time for meeting with God. Rather it's an opportunity for us to teach our children how to connect with their Creator, so they can approach Him on their own throughout their lives.

"Believer, be much in solitary prayer, especially in times of trial," says Charles H. Spurgeon in *Morning and Evening: Daily Readings*. "Family prayer, social prayer, prayer in the Church, will not suffice; these are very precious, but the best beaten spice will smoke in your censer in your private devotions where no ear hears but God's."

While I enjoy it when my family gathers to pray or read the Bible together, I find the most joy when my children seek God on their own—such as when my eleven-year-old son shares a Scripture verse he's chosen to memorize, or my thirteen-year-old daughter asks questions about a Bible passage she's been reading, or my sixteen-year-old son lines his computer monitor with sticky notes on which he's written out his favorite Bible verses.

It is then I realize that "devotions" are great as a set-apart time for families, but the specific word has even more meaning when it refers to a child's dedication, affection, and zeal for their Lord.

## BONUS MATERIAL

***Our five generations—GIs, Silents, Boomers, Xers and Millennials—have lived during the fastest moving century the world has ever known. During the past hundred years we walked on the moon, used the atom bomb and discovered the secrets of DNA. Television, the Internet and cell phones turned the planet into a global village.***[140]

# 23

# I Wanna Break Free

## Freeing Your Children from the World's Idols

***I want to break free from your lies....***

*Queen, The Works, 1984, Hollywood*

Every year billions of dollars are spent by advertisers to make us believe that what we have and who we are aren't enough. That we need something "better"—looks, food, toys, fun. You name it.

I'm as guilty as the rest when it comes to getting caught up in what the world offers. I'm quick to whip out my VISA card and slow to distinguish my needs from my wants.

And it's not only "things" that draw me—just the other day I took my daughter to get her hair cut and found myself eagerly flipping through the pages of *People* magazine—catching up on who's dating whom and who's wearing what, and lapping up those voyeuristic photos of glamorous stars caught in their sweatpants and ball caps while shopping at the grocery store.

When I take the time to think about it, I realize how silly this draw is. The people we idolize are simply people, after all. The "stuff" we desire is nothing more than man's attempt to create something beautiful and worthwhile. The successes we strive after are limited in scope and nature.

So why do we get caught up in worshiping the world's idols? And more important, how can we keep our kids from falling into the same trap?

## My Take On It

"The overwhelming level of distraction presents a big challenge to us as Christians—a challenge to focus not on worldly sound bites but on the quiet, unassuming voice of God. How do we hear Him in the maelstrom? And how do we get our children to distinguish His voice from all the others vying for their attention? It's a whole new ballgame for parents in this multimedia-driven age."

**—Judy, New York**
**Born in 1965, mother of two**

"In my struggle to give my kids the advantages in life, I hear God saying to me: 'On the day Jesus was born, Mary only had love to give to her brand-new baby. That's it! No warm house, no fancy car, and no brand-name clothing.' If the love of a mother is enough for our Savior, then surely today's children don't need too much more than that."

**—Kristy, Texas**
**Born in 1971, mother of three**

# Would I Lie To You?

***Now would I say something that wasn't true?***

EURYTHMICS, BE YOURSELF TONIGHT, 1985, LEGACY RECORDS

When it comes down to it, the things the world offers are no better than cheap trinkets found in bubble-gum vending machines. To needy people who seek hope, happiness, and peace, the world's offerings are counterfeit. And like $100 bills reproduced on a color copier, they may look good…but they have no true worth.

To make matters worse, the world is filled with posers who try to gain our attention by playing on our fears, seducing our senses, and driving us to strive for something unattainable apart from God. The trick to counteracting these attempts is learning to sift through the lies—and teaching our children to do the same.

Parents and children are being assaulted all the time, not only by the media, but by society in general. We need to look beyond the lies to the True Source. No matter who sells what, in reality we are being assaulted by the deceiver, whose greatest desire is to cause discontentment in our souls.

You can help your child find freedom from the world's idols when you teach them the following truths:

## 1. Not every thought that comes to our mind is from us.

Most of the ungodly thoughts that enter our minds are from the father of lies who dares to speak to us. *The Handbook of Bible Application* says:

> The Bible describes Satan as the deceiver. The devil is not a symbol or legend; he is very real. Originally Satan was an angel of God, but through his pride, he became corrupt. The devil is God's enemy and he constantly tries to hinder God's work, but he is limited by God's

power and can do only what he is permitted to do (Job 1:6–2:8). The name Satan means "adversary" or "accuser."[141]

The problem comes when we not only listen to the thoughts, lies, and accusations from the deceiver, but also embrace them. Satan craftily drops thoughts into our minds, and we accept them as our own.

*What I really need is...*
*What would make me happy is...*
*My life would be better if...*

We could finish those thoughts ten times over:

*...to lose twenty pounds.*
*...for my husband to pay more attention to me.*
*...I owned a nicer car or more stylish clothes.*

The same thoughts assault our kids: "I'd be happy if that boy in class liked me...if I had my own iPod...if I were taller...thinner...had different color hair...if I were better at sports."

The irony is that we have no need of the world's idols once we realize how precious we are to the Creator of the universe. To Him, we are "fearfully and wonderfully made." We don't need to look or act differently in order to find joy. We don't need more stuff to find peace. Instead, we need to see ourselves as God sees us. We need to combat the deceiver's lies with God's truth.

Here are some of these truths personalized:

- The Lord loves *me* with an everlasting love (Jeremiah 31:3).
- The Lord rejoices over *me* with singing and dancing (Zephaniah 3:17).
- Because I trust in Jesus, *I* am holy and blameless in God's eyes (Ephesians 1:3–11).

- *I* am precious in the sight of God (Isaiah 43:4).
- *I* am the apple of God's eye (Zechariah 2:8).
- *I* am forgiven, perfected forever, and free from condemnation because of what Jesus did for *me* (Romans 8:1; 2 Corinthians 5:21; Hebrews 10:14).
- Jesus will never leave *me* or abandon *me. I'm* his dear child (Matthew 28:20; John 14:18).[142]

What else could we possibly need or desire from the world when we cling to these?

### 2. Work to equalize the pressure inside our kids' souls.

Authors Richard and Renee Durfield relate this story in *Raising Pure Kids in an Impure World:*

> In April 1963, the American nuclear submarine *Thresher* disappeared about two hundred miles off the coast of New England. Radio contact was lost as the vessel underwent deep submergence tests. The ensuing attempts to contact and then locate the *Thresher* were all in vain.
>
> What happened? Apparently the submarine had traveled deeper than it was pressurized to go. The pressure of the waters on the outside simply exceeded the cabin pressure on the inside, and the vessel's walls collapsed. As a result, 129 sailors were lost.
>
> Our children—and we ourselves, for that matter—are like that submarine. The external pressures against self-control never let up, and in fact they increase as our culture descends deeper and deeper into immorality. If the internal pressure is unequal to the external—if there's not something strong enough inside them that says no to temptation—then our young people too will collapse. The combined weight of hormones, media messages, and peer pressure will simply overwhelm them.[143]

The internal strength is built up as our children learn God's Word and discover how to incorporate it into their lives:

> Evil people and impostors will flourish. They will go on deceiving others, and they themselves will be deceived. But you must remain faithful to the things you have been taught.... All Scripture is inspired by God and is useful to teach us what is true and to make us realize what is wrong in our lives. (2 Timothy 3:13–16, NLT)

The messages of the world will cause our children to cave under its pressure unless a stronger force is at work in our children's souls. You can impart this stronger force, God's Word, through Scripture memorization and by applying truth to everyday life.

### 3. Realize God's desire is not that we live apart from the world, but to serve Him in it.

John Fischer writes in *Finding God Where You Least Expect Him*:

> Those are revolutionary words: the Word made flesh. Christ came in the flesh, and in doing so, announced to us all that the flesh is not the problem. Our humanity is not the problem. Our material existence is not the problem. God is not going to do away with our humanity and turn us all into odd-looking Martians or wisps of spiritual ghosts floating around the universe, No, he's redeeming us body, soul, and spirit. He wants the whole thing...There's nothing wrong with the package it's just that sin twisted its focus away from God and onto ourselves. Redemption in Christ through his death and resurrection can reestablish our focus and put us right with ourselves and the world around us.[144]

To add to that, Romans 14:17–18 says:

> It's what God does with your life as he sets it right, puts it together, and completes it with joy. Your task is to single-mindedly serve Christ. Do that and you'll kill two birds with one stone: pleasing the God above you and proving your worth to the people around you. (*The Message*)

It's only through Christ that we can live in the world and not be overwhelmed by it. As this verse says, our task is to single-mindedly serve Christ. When we do that, God will take care of us and our place in the world.

### 4. Study the things the world attempts to glorify...and compare those things to God.

Ask your children to list the things the world tries to glorify: athletic accomplishments, beauty, youth, money, power, things, and acclaim. Then take time to compare these things with the living God. How do they compare? Which are lasting? Which will fade through the years? And in contrast, Who will never change or fade?

> Yes, they knew God, but they wouldn't worship him as God or even give him thanks. And they began to think up foolish ideas of what God was like. The result was that their minds became dark and confused. Claiming to be wise, they became utter fools instead. And instead of worshiping the glorious, ever-living God...they worshiped the things God made but not the Creator himself, who is to be praised forever. (Romans 1:21–23, 25, NLT)

### 5. Remind your children who will be around to satisfy us in the long run.

Ask your children what things they'd want most if they had unlimited resources. A new house? New car? Bigger, better toys? Then ask them to think about how long those things can truly satisfy. A day? A week? A year? Only God will always be around to give us the satisfaction of our hearts' desires.

> I will remember the deeds of the LORD; yes, I will remember your miracles of long ago. I will meditate on all your works and consider all your mighty deeds. (Psalm 77:11–12)

Instead of focusing on "more" from the world, take time to thank God that He is enough. Share your thoughts with your kids, and ask them to share with you. Then, together, place your hope in our God who knows the future.

When it comes down to it, freeing our children from the world's idols centers around focusing on the one true God. The things we worship today aren't like the gold and silver idols of times past...but they require just as much devotion from our hearts.

When we take time to really compare God's glory with the things that vie for our attention, we realize that what the world offers is no comparison. Not even close.

## My Take On It

"Part of my daughters' schoolwork is practicing handwriting by using Bible verses. It's amazing how the Word of God, read by a child, can give clarity in the midst of a difficult moment."

**—Amy, Georgia**
**Born in 1970, mother of three**

"Contentment is a huge challenge in a world that preaches we should always want more. A bigger house, a better car, a perfect job, the ideal child, the world's best marriage. Everything is disposable. It is only as I seek God that I am truly content with the life I have."

**—Cara, Indiana**
**Born in 1974, mother of two**

## BONUS MATERIAL

The born-again movement represented a part of the upsurge of evangelicalism in the 1970s. Between 1963 and 1978, the percentage of Americans claiming to have been "born again" and having personally experienced salvation rose from 24 to 40. By the end of the 1970s, more than 50 million Americans claimed to be evangelicals. Local congregations played a part in evangelicalism's growing strength, as did church-related colleges, publishing firms, and the denominations sponsoring or supporting them. Evangelicals regarded their Gospel-centered emphasis and clear-cut moral codes, along with their belief in conversion experiences, as standing in sharp contrast to what they perceived to be the consequences of "secular humanism." Evangelicals and fundamentalists, who were more rigid in their Biblical literalism than evangelicals and harsher in their criticisms of societal changes, blamed secular humanism for increases in teenage sexual activity, alcohol and drug abuse, and discipline problems in public schools.[145]

# 24 Caught Up in You

## Getting Filled with God

***You're the one that's got me down on my knees....***

***.38 Special, Special Forces, 1982, A & M***

What I remember most about religion during my growing-up years is crazy, confused messages. Even though I attended church, I also grew up in a small town in Northern California on the side of Mt. Shasta. There were religious zealots everywhere—thousands of hippie seekers who journeyed to what they considered a "sacred mountain." There were harmonic convergences, sit-ins, and everything in between. And I've discovered this "new way of thinking" wasn't just a California thing, but a common theme during the Gen Xers' coming-of-age era.

Victor Bondi has this to say about that era:

> The New Age movement found its way into the mainstream of society in the mid-80s. Included in its tenets were beliefs in reincarnation, spiritual healing, out-of-body experiences, meditation, yoga, astrology, and the supernatural or extraterrestrial. New Age music, speakers, and books became widely available. In 1988, there were more than 2,500 New Age bookstores, 25,000 titles in print, and annual sales amounting to $1 billion.[146]

Yet instead of shrugging off these beliefs, many people from our generation explored them and even embraced them. And if we didn't believe in these things ourselves, we knew better than to speak against someone else's claim.

The authors of *Boomers, Xers, and Other Strangers* write:

> Growing up in a society that emphasized the rights of various minority groups, [Gen Xers] tend to be more tolerant and accepting of individuals of various backgrounds and lifestyles. Their exposure to so many different beliefs and philosophies, plus their commitment to tolerance, has made it difficult for them to believe that there are any absolute truths in life to live by.[147]

Yet for most of us reading this book, we've found the answer. And it's an answer that should transform us inside and out.

# Hungry Eyes

***I've got this feelin' that won't subside....***

**ERIC CARMEN, *DIRTY DANCING* SOUNDTRACK, 1987, RCA**

As I write this, our church just finished moving into a new building. And even before our first church service was held there, we already had tenants—a bird's nest filled with babies, protected by their faithful mother.

My thirteen-year-old daughter, Leslie, had the opportunity to watch the baby birds as they hungrily awaited their mother's return. "Mom, they have such long necks," she reported. "And their mouths were wide open, waiting for food."

It reminded me of something I'd read earlier that morning: "Open wide your mouth and I will fill it" (Psalm 81:10). And it made me realize that though I pray for God to sustain me, rarely do I truly hunger for it. I want much, but I expect little. I know God loves me, but rarely do I live with confidence that He is my bountiful benefactor.

> Praise the LORD, O my soul, and forget not all his benefits...who satisfies your desires with good things. (Psalm 103:2, 5)

God alone can satisfy. He can replenish every hungry, weary soul, gratifying those who are faithful to Him. We know this; yet how does it look to be long-necked and widemouthed, open to God's filling?

I don't know about you, but there are times when I turn to other things in hopes of finding satisfaction. Sometimes my longing drives me to the mall or to the refrigerator or searching the Internet for great travel deals. The only problem is even after I've spent my money, increased my waistline, or soaked in the sun, I still feel empty.

But I'm learning what I need to be truly filled. Sometimes that means escaping to the quiet of my room, curling up in a ball on my bed, and praying to God for strength and peace. Other times it's opening my Bible and filling my mind with God's Word. I especially love reading the Gospels of Matthew, Mark, Luke, and John, paying attention to Jesus' love for His followers. I imagine myself there, the one being touched, spoken to, embraced. Still other times, I find a praise CD and let worship tunes fill the room. Even if I'm paying bills or playing with my kids, I close my eyes every few minutes and imagine God seated on His heavenly throne, surrounded by angels, accepting my praise.

These things seem simple, but their impact is huge. They represent my need and prove God's willingness to supply. And now I have a new image to picture in my mind as I read, or pray, or sing. One of God approaching with care, noting my wide mouth and long neck, and satisfying my desires with good things.

A. W. Tozer speaks of God's love for us in *Whatever Happened to Worship*:

> The living God has been willing to reveal Himself to our seeking hearts. He would have us know and understand that He is all love and that those who trust Him need never know anything but that love.... This is the best of good news; God loves us for ourselves. He values our love more than He values galaxies of new created worlds.[148]

It's then that I'm filled—when my heart can grasp the idea that God values my love most of all.

## My Take On It

"How can we expect our children to listen to and really hear us if we are not living examples by truly hearing and following God? 'Do as He says, not as I do'? I don't think so. Children are drawn to God by parents who have a real relationship with the Lord. If we show how important that relationship is to us, they'll want it as well."

**—Judy, New York**
**Born in 1965, mother of two**

> "I love to sing. I've found that when I'm struggling the most, a children's Bible song or an old hymn is a perfect way to get my mind off the circumstances and back onto what really matters. For me, that's one way God really speaks within the chaos."
>
> **—Amy, Georgia**
> **Born in 1970, mother of three**

# Heart and Soul

***Give a little bit of love to grow....***

***T'PAU, BRIDGE OF SPIES, 1996, VIRGIN***

"One response was given by the innkeeper when Mary and Joseph wanted to find a room where the Child could be born. The innkeeper was not hostile; he was not opposed to them, but his inn was crowded; his hands were full; his mind was preoccupied," says evangelist Billy Graham. "This is the answer that millions are giving today. Like a Bethlehem innkeeper, they cannot find room for Christ. All the accommodations in their hearts are already taken up by other crowding interests. Their response is not atheism. It is not defiance. It is preoccupation and the feeling of being able to get on reasonably well without Christianity."

As a parent, one of the best things we can do for our children is to find room for Christ. Not allowing our hearts to be crowded or our hands to be full. Not allowing our minds to be preoccupied. It's allowing ourselves to find intimacy with our Lord.

And what does intimacy provide? You will find a few of the answers below. And if you long for this type of intimacy, there are also suggestions for you to connect with God.

**1. Strong, calm balance.** Oswald Chambers writes:

> Once we get intimate with Jesus we are never lonely and we never lack for understanding or compassion. We can continually pour out our hearts to Him without being perceived as overly emotional or pitiful. The Christian who is truly intimate with Jesus will never draw attention to himself but will only show the evidence of a life where Jesus is completely in control. This is the outcome of allowing Jesus to satisfy every area of life to its depth. The picture resulting from such a life is that of the strong, calm balance that our Lord gives to those who are intimate with Him.[149]

Do you feel this strong, calm balance? If not, follow the suggestions Chambers talked about:

- Take a few minutes a day to pour out your heart to God.
- Don't worry about feeling overly emotional or pitiful.
- Ask God to satisfy every area of your life to its depths.
- Count on the strong, calm balance our Lord gives to those who are intimate with Him.

**2. A heart to worship and obey.** Worship is the way we express intimacy in our relationship with God. Richard J. Foster says, "Just as worship begins in holy expectancy, it ends in holy obedience. If worship does not propel us into greater obedience, it has not been worship."

- Spend a few minutes worshiping God.
- If you have a hard time obeying in a certain matter, worship some more.

**3. Desire.** Intimacy with God begins when we confess, "My God..." He's not "some big guy up there, somewhere," but a personal God who cares for me.

Here is a prayer that proved David's heart and desire for God…and one you can repeat to prove yours.

> O God, you are my God; I earnestly search for you. My soul thirsts for you; my whole body longs for you in this parched and weary land where there is no water.
>
> I have seen you in your sanctuary and gazed upon your power and glory. Your unfailing love is better to me than life itself; how I praise you!
>
> I will honor you as long as I live, lifting up my hands to you in prayer. You satisfy me more than the richest of foods. I will praise you with songs of joy.
>
> I lie awake thinking of you, meditating on you through the night.
>
> I think how much you have helped me; I sing for joy in the shadow of your protecting wings.
>
> I follow close behind you; your strong right hand holds me securely. (Psalm 63:1–8, NLT)

So why is growing in intimacy with God so important? Maybe the statistics at the beginning of this chapter will clue you in.

There are a lot of religious zealots out there. The New Age movement that came to prominence during our formative years is only one of many lures. There are people, causes, and false promises working to draw your children away from a deep relationship with a living God. And the only thing that will keep your children true to their faith is an intimate relationship with Jesus—one they learn from your example, but form for themselves.

> So, my dear Christian friends, companions in following this call to the heights, take a good hard look at Jesus. He's the centerpiece of everything we believe, faithful in everything God gave him to do. (Hebrews 3:1–2, *The Message*)

The deeper you get in your relationship with Jesus, the more they will see it as something real. To echo Oswald Chambers' excerpt, "The Christian who is truly intimate with Jesus will never draw attention to himself but will only show the evidence of a life where Jesus is completely in control."

This evidence is just what your children need in a world that has plenty of options. Won't you go deeper today...for you and for them?

## My Take On It

"I am one of the Gen Xers who grew up in a wonderful, godly home. I don't feel I need to give my kids more than I had, but I do want to pass on the godly characteristics my parents taught me. And I want my sons to establish their relationship with God sooner than I did.

"Yes, I know when I became a Christian and I never rebelled, but I never really established the daily walk with God. I was a comfortable Christian who served God more than most, but I didn't have an in-depth, daily reliance upon Him. Today does matter! It matters what I'm modeling to my kids today!"

**—Scott, Washington**
**Born in 1968, father of two**

## Bonus Material

**The percentage of Americans who "completely agree" that "prayer is an important part of my daily life" rose from 41 percent in 1987 to 53 percent in 1997, an increase of twelve percentage points. Those who "completely agree" that they never doubt the existence of God rose eleven points in the same ten years.**[150]

# 25 LIVIN' ON A Prayer

## Prayer Changes Things

***Take my hand and we'll make it—I swear....***

BON JOVI, SLIPPERY WHEN WET, 1986, MERCURY

More than anything, parenting takes courage. There is no "going with the flow." No "just trying to slide by" when it comes to raising kids.

"I think I could have faked this whole Christianity thing if I didn't have kids," my friend Joanna confessed as we talked on the phone this morning. "It's impossible to go through these parenting years without being totally dependent on God."

Sometimes I imagine the fear Joshua must have felt when facing the walls of Jericho with a band of nomadic shepherds. Oh, how he must have prayed as he viewed the seemingly insurmountable obstacle before him.

> Be strong and courageous, for you will lead my people to possess all the land I swore to give their ancestors. Be strong and very courageous.... Study this Book of the Law continually. Meditate on it day and night so you may be sure to obey all that is written in it. Only

> then will you succeed. I command you—be strong and courageous! Do not be afraid or discouraged. For the LORD your God is with you wherever you go. (Joshua 1:6–9, NLT)

In those two verses, God tells Joshua to be strong and courageous three times. First, because Joshua was quaking in his boots. Second, because Joshua needed the reminder to meditate on God's Word. And third, because God wanted to remind Joshua that He was in control. No matter how intimidating the situation, God was present.

This story of Joshua illustrates three things.

1. We need to look to God in prayer.
2. We need to look at the Word for the courage to be strong.
3. We need to realize God *is* in control.

Through a clear visual that proved the Israelites couldn't win on their own (marching around the wall, blowing trumpets), God showed Joshua and His people that He would win the victory for them. We need to approach God in the same manner, knowing as we enter the uphill battle of raising kids, we must trust the success to Him.

Sometimes this is hard to see. I'm sure tramping around walls was not the answer Joshua envisioned, but we know God doesn't always answer our prayers as we hoped or expected. In *My Utmost for His Highest*, Chambers writes, "God answers prayer in the best way, not sometimes, but every time."[151]

Prayer equals pleading one's case before God, getting God's perspective, and gaining confidence and courage—no matter the situation. In raising kids in this day and age, we need to take all our needs before God, just as Joshua did, leaving the results to Him. Dr. Tim Kimmel writes in *Grace Based Parenting*:

> Sometimes [God] answers our prayers with answers like "No" or "Wait" or "Later." When he does it's because He is working to make us better and stronger and to draw us closer to Him. He has a bigger plan that

this setback fits into. Children need to have a hope in His love that enables them to trust in His character while walking down these painful corridors of their lives. For the child facing these crises, the grace that has surrounded him, the love he's been shown, and the character of the parents who gave him that grace and love provide a natural springboard for him to rest in God's final answer to his pleas. It helps him hope when everyone else would give up.[152]

That's what prayer is...living hope that God's answer is always best.

## My Take On It

"I struggle with prayer. I don't have time to pray. I don't have the energy. I don't know what to say. I fall asleep. How on earth can I pray with all of this NOISE?!?! Who gets up at 5 a.m. to pray? Do they ever sleep?

"All good excuses, right? The fact is, I am not committed to prayer. I pray as a last resort (after I tried to fix the problem myself, after I am angry and frustrated and don't know what to do next, after I searched the entire house for my car keys...twice). My biggest struggle with prayer is my own laziness."

**—Michelle H., Ohio**
**Born in 1971, mother of four**

"Right now my daughter is only fifteen months old, and prayer is kind of hard for her to understand; however, we do pray before every meal and before she goes to bed. She knows when we put her in her chair, we're going to pray so she puts her hands together. I didn't grow up in a Christian home, so I want my daughter brought up differently than I was."

**—Jennifer J., Tennessee**
**Born in 1974, mother of one**

## Save a Prayer

***But we can call it paradise....***

**Duran Duran, Rio, 1982, Capitol/EMI Records**

Parenting is hard. Parenting is rewarding. Parenting wears me out. Parenting fills me with joy. Parenting presents us with every emotion…and some we didn't even know existed. So what do we do with all these emotions?

> The first thing I want you to do is pray. Pray every way you know how, for everyone you know…. This is the way our Savior God wants us to live. (1 Timothy 2:1, 3, *The Message*)

Of course, there is no such thing as "one prayer fits all." During our parenting journey we will pray various ways at different times, but as one of my friends taught me, one of the best ways to pray is to pray the *Word of God*.

There are tons of books on prayer, dozens of resources, but really all it takes is sitting down with verses such as these, praying them out loud or in your heart, and tacking on your own personal message at the end. It's that easy!

Here are some Scriptures for your parenting journey. Some have been personalized for you. And of course, feel free to add your own Scriptures to this list as God speaks to you!

### 1. Prayers of need.

- "Lord, I cast all my cares upon You, knowing You will sustain me. You will never let me, Your righteous one, fall" (from Psalm 55:22).
- "Lord, I am blessed when I trust in You, and when my hope is in You. For I will be like a tree planted by the waters, spreading out my roots by the river. I will not fear when heat comes and my leaf will be green. I will not be anxious in the year of drought, and I will not cease from yielding fruit" (from Jeremiah 17:7–8).

- "Lord, You say in Your word when I call on You, You will answer me and tell me great and unsearchable things I do not know" (from Jeremiah 33:3).
- "Lord, help me hold unswervingly to the hope I profess, for You who promised are faithful" (from Hebrews 10:23).
- "Lord, I acknowledge You, and I press on to acknowledge You more. As surely as the sun rises, You will appear. You will come to me like the winter rains, like the spring rains that water the earth" (from Hosea 6:3).
- "Lord, I do not fear, for You are with me. I will not be dismayed, for You are my God. You will strengthen me and help me. You will uphold me with Your righteous right hand" (from Isaiah 41:10).

### 2. Prayers of thanksgiving.

- "LORD, my God, you have done many miracles for us. Your plans for us are too numerous to list. If I tried to recite all your wonderful deeds, I would never come to the end of them" (Psalm 40:5, NLT).
- "Oh, the depth of the riches of the wisdom and knowledge of God! How unsearchable Your judgments, and Your paths beyond tracing out!" (from Romans 11:33).
- "Lord, I will thank You forever, because of what You have done. In the presence of the faithful I will proclaim Your name, for it is good" (from Psalm 52:9).
- "I will give thanks to your name for your unfailing love and faithfulness, because your promises are backed by all the honor of your name. When I pray, you answer me; you encourage me by giving me the strength I need" (Psalm 138:2–3, NLT).

### 3. Prayers for seeking families.

- "Lord, today I pray the words of Jesus, 'O Father, Lord of heaven and earth, thank you for hiding the truth from those who think themselves so wise and clever, and for revealing it to the childlike. Yes, Father, it pleased you to do it this way!'" (from Matthew 11:25).
- "The LORD protects those of childlike faith; I was facing death, and then he saved me. Now I can rest again, for the LORD has been so good to me" (Psalm 116:6–7, NLT).
- "The living, the living, we thank You, as I do this day. May we mothers and fathers make known to our children Your faithfulness" (from Isaiah 38:19).
- "May our sons flourish in their youth like well-nurtured plants. May our daughters be like graceful pillars, carved to beautify a palace" (Psalm 144:12, NLT).

### 4. Prayers for generations.

- "Lord, may our generation tell our children of Your mighty acts. We will meditate on Your majestic, glorious splendor and Your wonderful miracles" (from Psalm 145:4–5).
- "You are the Lord our God. Your rule is seen throughout the land. You always stand by your covenant—the commitment You made to a thousand generations" (from Psalm 105:7–8).
- "O Lord, You are good. Your unfailing love continues forever, and Your faithfulness continues to each generation" (from Psalm 100:5).
- "Lord, through all the generations you have been our home! Before the mountains were created, before you made the earth and the world, you are God, without beginning or end" (Psalm 90:1–2, NLT).

## My Take On It

"Prayer helps me to remember the big picture and that my perception of things isn't always accurate, since I see 'as through a glass dimly.' My husband and I pray over our son every night before he goes to bed. Doing so helps me remember that God has his life planned out for him and the little things that seem so big are really very, very small compared to God's plan for our son. The same thing applies in the prayer time my husband and I have together. It's just so good to connect with God and focus on His thoughts."

**—Jenn, New York**
**Born in 1972, mother of one**

"When there is a skinned knee or a yard scuffle, I gather my kids together and we pray. It's amazing how well this diffuses both the bickering and the need for the bandage (which I don't have because the baby wanted them to be tiny toilet rafts that morning)."

**—Cheryl, Illinois**
**Born in 1969, mother of three**

"If I didn't have my friends and mentors praying for me I wouldn't be where I am today. Since I was not raised in a Christian environment, I never knew how valuable prayer was as a child. Now I truly get it, need it, want it, can't live without it."

**—Kristy, Texas**
**Born in 1971, mother of three**

## The Listening Side of Prayer

While it is important to pray with both pleas and thanksgiving, we must not forget the other side to prayer—the listening side. The King James Version translates Proverbs 29:18 this way:

> Where there is no vision, the people perish: but he that keepeth the law, happy is he.

From this verse we take note that the lack of vision or guidance is on the part of the people. Whether they don't know how to listen and have shut their ears, or they simply do not want to accept what is given to them, their refusal leads to their destruction.

So many times I've heard people say, "I wish God would just speak to me and tell me what to do," or "I wish He'd give me a sign." There are times I've desired the same thing. But lately I've come to realize that even a sign, or vision, or some other type of divine guidance will do *no good* if my heart is not prepared to follow God at any cost.

*What would I do if I heard from God? How would I respond?*

It takes an eager heart and a tender conscience (as described in Proverbs 28:14, NLT) to understand and to follow. A clearer picture of this is seen with Jesus' interaction with the crowds who sought him out:

> When he saw the crowds, he had compassion on them, because they were harassed and helpless, like sheep without a shepherd. (Matthew 9:36–38)

It's sad to realize many of those who sought Jesus had the opportunity to see and hear Him...and still walked away disillusioned. It's not enough to hear the voice of Christ. It's what we *do* with it that matters.

Here is another prayer for you as a parent:

Lord, give me a tender conscience, a heart eager to accept divine guidance, and feet prepared to follow. I pray the same for my children. Amen.

*Jesus desires to speak to you today.*
*Get your walking shoes ready.*

## Prayer for Us

Finally, I'm offering one more prayer, not only for yourself and your family, but for all Gen X parents. God has called *us* to parent during this time in history. If you feel led, copy this prayer and pray it daily. Pray that God will unify us and unite our hearts and vision for this generation of children. Trust that He will be faithful to do so.

It is no coincidence you're reading these words. This prayer is being prayed for you, too.

> I pray for you constantly, asking God, the glorious Father of our Lord Jesus Christ, to give you **spiritual wisdom** and **understanding**, so that you might **grow in your knowledge of God**. I pray that your **hearts will be flooded with light** so that you can **understand the wonderful future** he has promised to those he called. I want you to **realize what a rich and glorious inheritance** he has given to his people.
>
> "I pray that you will **begin to understand the incredible greatness of his power** for us who believe him. This is the same mighty power that raised Christ from the dead and seated him in the place of honor at God's right hand in the heavenly realms. Now he is far above any ruler or authority or power or leader or anything else in this world or in the world to come. (Ephesians 1:16–21, NLT)

## DO YOU REMEMBER?

- John Lennon was assassinated on December 8, 1980.
- Prince Charles married Lady Diana Spencer on July 29, 1981.
- The *Challenger* space shuttle exploded on takeoff on January 28, 1986.
- A lone protester stood in front of tanks on Tiananmen Square on June 4, 1989.
- The Berlin Wall came down on November 9, 1989.
- Nelson Mandela was released from jail on February 11, 1990.
- There were riots in Los Angeles after the Rodney King trial verdict on April 30, 1992.

## OTHER THINGS I REMEMBER...

- Molly Ringwald
- *Space Invaders*
- Moon boots
- *St. Elmo's Fire*
- "Don't hate me because I'm beautiful"
- Obsession, Poison, and Eternity perfume and cologne
- *Howard the Duck* (I think this takes the prize for worst movie ever made)
- Depeche Mode
- *Fantasy Island*
- Punk rock
- Rainbow shirts (Add a unicorn and it was even cooler)
- Velcro wallets

**—Jeanette, Nevada**
**Born in 1967, mother of two**

# 26 FAITH

## Faith, Not Fear

***But I'll wait for something more....***

*George Michael, Faith, 1987, Columbia*

As Gen Xers, we grew up learning to fear the world. The authors of *Boomers, Xers, and Other Strangers* write:

> In the 1980s, the world's attitude toward the United States was changing. The Iran hostage situation showed that even a small country, one that most had never heard of, could create a problem we couldn't solve. We began to see the impact of the personal computer and other inventions that ushered us into a high-tech society. One of the negative factors was the discovery and epidemic spread of AIDS. Drug use increased significantly, causing the president to appoint a drug czar to wage a war on drugs.[153]

Of course, there were other things that hit closer to home. Victor Bondi reminds us of something else that impacted our childhood:

> The problem of the abduction of children also became highly publicized as the pictures of missing children began showing up on milk

cartons in the mid-'80s. (That had to have an effect on the children who saw them every morning as they ate their cereal.) In 1985, more than one million children were reported missing; 6,000 of them were abducted by strangers.[154]

I remember the fears of being home at night, sure there was someone outside trying to get in. (I'm sure the horror movies I watched didn't help.) But there were also fears of nuclear war, famine, and of losing my family. I thought I'd dealt with those things when I grew up. I thought I'd come to have faith in God in all things...but have I?

Even today, I don't let my children answer the door when I'm not home. I also don't let them answer the phone or tell anyone they're home alone. They can't go out on a bike ride without my knowing exactly where they will be and when they'll be back. I check their e-mails and have passwords set up on their Internet access. I check out every book they read and every television show they watch.

*Have I taught them to fear too much?*

I didn't think so until I heard the story of the rescued Boy Scout in Utah. Though rescuers had come close to him many times, he at first hid from them instead of seeking to be rescued. Why? His parents had told him never to go to strangers. Whoa.

So I ask myself again, *Have I put too much emphasis on fear instead of faith?*

Dr. Teresa Whitehurst writes in *How Would Jesus Raise a Child*:

> Jesus knew that losing faith in God—despair—leads to terrible things. Jesus knew that when human beings encounter adversity or become fatigued, they can forget to pray and go back to relying on their own resources. Once this happens, despair sets in like a rude, uninvited houseguest.[155]

Hope is the opposite of despair. Faith is the opposite of fear. But can we find a happy medium in raising cautious kids while at the same time providing them with trust in a completely-in-control God?

After all, instead of the rude, uninvited houseguest of despair, wouldn't we rather have the Lord of hope and truth as the center of our children's lives?

## Where's Our Faith?

In 1987, the song "Faith" became George Michael's first #1 solo. Six singles from the album of the same name hit the Top Five, garnering him a Best Album Grammy. And while the words "Yes, I've gotta have faith..." flow through my mind whenever I hear that word, it wasn't until I looked up the lyrics that I realized what George Michael was singing about.

In essence, the song is about a person who is offering her body to him—yet he knows she will steal his heart away and throw it to the floor. So despite the fact that he needs someone to hold him, someone to show him devotion, *he's going to wait for something more*. A pretty amazing concept, if you ask me.

> What is faith? It is the confident assurance that what we hope for is going to happen. It is the evidence of things we cannot yet see. God gave his approval to people in days of old because of their faith. (Hebrews 11:1–2, NLT)

I have no idea how long George Michael's faith lasted, or how long he held out waiting for that "something more" (or even if he ever did). But I do know that in our daily life as parents, having this type of faith is crucial.

Faith means not only trusting in what Christ did in the past for our salvation or believing in what He will do in the future. Faith is also trusting in what He can do for us in the present, as parents. And what He can do for our kids.

> A righteous person will live by faith. But I will have no pleasure in anyone who turns away. (Hebrews 10:38, NLT)

The word *faith* here is translated as "persuasion, assurance, belief." And the words *turn away* mean to "withdraw, shrink back, shun."

Applying this to our parenting journey:

> A righteous parent will live with persuasion, assurance, and belief in God's provision. But [God] will have no pleasure in anyone who withdraws, shrinks back or shuns Him.

Today, which will you choose—to turn to God or turn away? Not in the sense of your salvation but in your *situation*, whether it is teething, potty training, discipline problems, or snotty attitudes. Or...even bigger stuff like terrorists, flu outbreaks, and kidnappers. Or...the "world" that tries to exert its influence at every turn, desiring to lead our children astray—threatening not only their lives, but their very souls.

John Fischer writes in *Fearless Faith*:

> [After 9/11] we discovered our sense of safety was no more than a myth, an illusion. But losing our illusion may not have been such a bad thing. It awakened us to reality, and even if that reality is painful, we are better off embracing it than lying to ourselves. In the same way, we need to wake up to the reality of the world we live in as Christians and realize that the safe Christian subculture we've been working so hard to build is an illusion as well. It's essential, in fact, for us to awaken to this truth. To think we are safe when we are not is to perpetuate a false security. I would suggest that we as Christians need to learn to *embrace* the danger of living in a dangerous world and trust not a safe subculture to protect us, but a praying Savior. Only then

can we go into the world as Christ has sent us: with hope and a fearless faith, and a mission to love, serve, and manifest the good news of Jesus Christ.[156]

Trusting in a praying Savior. I like that.

## My Take On It

"I pray all the time about parenting. Throughout the day, God gives me a lot of reminders about life, truth, reality. So much of what I experience as a parent happens inside my head, without much fact, which then leads to a lot of fear. God continues to work with me to keep me focused on what is right in front of me and how to deal with it.

"I also remember that it is through suffering and uncomfortable circumstances that we grow, which is helping me let go a little of the kids and let them experience life as it really is, not the Barney version."

**—Rene, Oklahoma**
**Born in 1972, mother of two**

"I was brought up in a Christian home where faith played a role in my upbringing. It has set an example for how I want to raise my daughter to be a serving daughter of our heavenly Father."

**—Lisa, Colorado**
**Born in 1977, mother of one**

## The Answer

The answer, of course, is to stand on God's promises. To believe God will do what He said He will do—for our culture, our safety, our families, our future, and our present.

And what does God promise to do? Here are a few things:

> [God] does not ignore those who cry to him for help. (Psalms 9:12, NLT)

> Your godliness will lead you forward, and the glory of the LORD will protect you from behind. Then when you call, the LORD will answer. "Yes, I am here," he will quickly reply. (Isaiah 58:8–9, NLT)

> For God has reserved a priceless inheritance for his children. It is kept in heaven for you, pure and undefiled, beyond the reach of change and decay. And God, in his mighty power, will protect you until you receive this salvation, because you are trusting him. (1 Peter 1:4–5, NLT)

> I created you and have cared for you since before you were born. I will be your God throughout your lifetime—until your hair is white with age. I made you, and I will care for you. I will carry you along and save you. (Isaiah 46:3–4, NLT)

Of course we believe in a victorious life eternal, but what about faith for a victorious life in the present?

> [Abraham] did not waver through unbelief regarding the promise of God, but was strengthened in his faith and gave glory to God, *being fully persuaded* that God had power to do what he had promised. (Romans 4:20–21)

What that boils down to is faith. *You've gotta have faith, faith, faith. Oh, you gotta have faith.*

George Michael might have never found his "something more," but we have:

> For at the right time Christ will be revealed from heaven by the blessed and only almighty God, the King of kings and Lord of lords. He alone can never die, and he lives in light so brilliant that no human can approach him. No one has ever seen him, nor ever will. To him be honor and power forever. Amen. (1 Timothy 6:15–16, NLT)

That is the Christ we have faith in…the one we worship and trust. That is the Christ who will protect and care for you and your family. He's all that and more!

So when parenting stirs up fears, that's when faith comes in. Faith in God's promise that He loves our children even more than we do and that He will take care of them.

Believe it. Trust it. Pray for this faith to be made real in your heart. And then pray for it to be made real in your children's hearts, too.

Believe it. Trust it. Pray for this faith to be made real in your heart. And then pray for it to be made real in your children's hearts, too.

Because no matter what obstacles we face as parents, and no matter what obstacles our kids will have to overcome, Christ will see us through. Just as He has done in the past. Just as He will do in the future. He is here to help, guide, and protect you today.

Now. This moment.

# Good-Bye

***Never close, never far, always there when I needed a friend....***

*Night Ranger, Seven Wishes, 1985, MCA Records*

When I started writing this book, I had the gut feeling that Gen Xers were different. I could sense it when I was around older parents, but I didn't realize—didn't know—until I started researching.

I have to admit that some of it was discouraging. I mean, who wants to hear that their generation was pretty much labeled as unable to achieve anything of importance? The authors of *Boomers, Xers, and Other Strangers* write:

> They're a group of tough individuals. They grew up in difficult financial times. They were being raised when the traditional family in America was deteriorating, but they held on, and they are ready to fight for their future.[157]

And we are fighting for it, aren't we? We may have been crossed out a while ago, but some of us have found *the* way to fight: with the cross of Christ. (So *take that*, all you who said we wouldn't amount to much!)

As I was researching there were some cool things I discovered, too. We are good parents. We are! And we are taking all the icky stuff from the past and turning it around to raise kids who love God. We are more balanced, more realistic, and more willing to turn to God than the generations who come before us—despite having more challenges.

Finally, one last thought concerning our generation's "given" name:

The letter *X* is the abbreviation for Christ. (It's the Greek letter *Chi.*) It's why people write *X-mas*—whether they know it or not. What a calling we have. What a great reminder that Christ has marked us as His own. Generation Christ's. Maybe God had His hand on our being named this, too.

Also, think about the marking *X*. What do you do when you agree with a document? You *X* the right box, and then you sign it. The *X* is a confirmation of your agreement.

There are a few places God talks about this type of agreement in His Word.

> Do what I say and you'll live well. My teaching is as precious as your eyesight—guard it! Write it out on the back of your hands; etch it on the chambers of your heart. (Proverbs 7:2–3, *The Message*)

> Place these words on your hearts. Get them deep inside you. Tie them on your hands and foreheads as a reminder. Teach them to your children. Talk about them wherever you are, sitting at home or walking in the street; talk about them from the time you get up in the morning until you fall into bed at night. Inscribe them on the doorposts and gates of your cities so that you'll live a long time, and your children with you, on the soil that God promised to give your ancestors for as long as there is a sky over the Earth. (Deuteronomy 11:18–21, *The Message*)

Etch God's Word...inscribe it...talk about it. *This* is what is going to make the difference in our generation. As you can see, God's Word was the foundation for every concept in this book. His truth is what I offered you in each chapter.

So will you do something with me? Will you accept this challenge to continue in the study of God's Word? To apply it to your parenting, and every other situation in your life?

Remember this game?

I will continue to apply God's Word to every part of my life. (Pick one. Mark it with an X and sign it.)

[ ] Yes

[ ] No

*Signature:* ______________________________

Now, prepare to do something else. Prepare not only to make your mark on the page; prepare to cross (make an *X* over) your heart.

We may have been a generation that was crossed out. But together we will confirm our agreement to God that we will inscribe His truth in our hearts.

Ready? One, two, three.

Cross.

## My Take On It

"X means to leave your mark. For instance, an X left on a treasure map is a guide to those searching for a treasure.

"We as parents leave our marks everywhere. Our children are our marks, the legacy we leave behind. With this understanding, I have to ask myself,

'What X am I leaving on my life's map? Where is it leading my children?'

"The letter X in 'Generation X' was not given to us by mistake. It was given to us as a reminder that we will be used to influence the current world and generations after us. We are to leave an X for others to follow; that X will lead them to Christ."

**—Stephanie, Ohio**
**Born in 1977, mother of two**

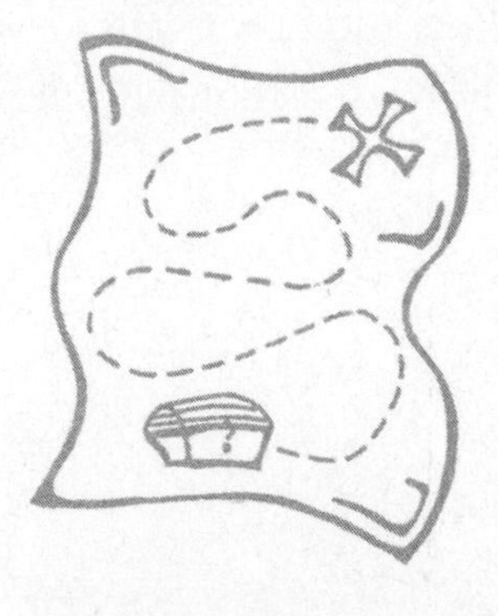

# Study Guide

## Digging Deeper

*I'm asking GOD for one thing,*
*only one thing:*
*To live with him in his house*
*my whole life long.*
*I'll contemplate his beauty;*
*I'll study at his feet.*

(Psalm 27:4, *The Message*)

## INTRODUCTION: I PROMISE YOU

1. Do you think our generation can be grouped as parents? Why?
2. What do you think our generation of parents can be characterized by?
3. What differences do you see between Gen X parents and parents of other generations?
4. Do these differences strengthen or hinder us as parents?

## 1 TIME AFTER TIME: DEPENDING ON GOD

1. God has determined the set times for each of us, and the exact places where we should live. How do you think living in this time and place has required you to seek Him? What things overwhelm you most about living in this day and age?
2. What words do you think God is speaking to our generation? Why do you think we require God now more than ever?
3. In what ways can you turn to God when you feel overwhelmed?
4. In what ways can good friends encourage you? How can you encourage others?

### Digging Deeper

**Isaiah 45:21-24** **Psalm 33:13-15**
**Isaiah 34:16-17** **Acts 3:19-20** **Isaiah 41:2-4**

## 2 I'M GONNA LIVE FOREVER: THE HEAVENLY REALITY

1. What is the challenge of "setting your mind on things above" during daily living?
2. What do you picture in your mind's eye when you imagine Christ seated at the right hand of God?
3. How do you turn your focus to God throughout the day?
4. In what ways can you help your kids see God's active hand in the world around us?

### Digging Deeper

**Psalm 16:11** **Mark 16:19**
**2 Corinthians 4:17-18** **Philippians 3:20-21** **Psalm 119:36-37**

## 3 I DON'T KNOW MUCH: PARENTING ADVICE OVERLOAD

1. Author Gregory Boyd said, "The fruit of the Spirit is not a goal we can and must seek to attain. Indeed, it is called the fruit *of the Spirit* precisely because it is the fruit *of the Spirit* and not the product of our own effort." Do you agree or disagree? Why?
2. In what ways can you yield to the Spirit? How can the Spirit's guidance help you as you parent?
3. When was a time you felt you were "walking in step with the Spirit"? What was the result?
4. Where does the best parenting advice you receive come from? Who do you listen to?

### Digging Deeper

**John 15:5** **John 15:16**
**Galatians 5:16-18** **1 Peter 4:6** **Ephesians 5:8-9**

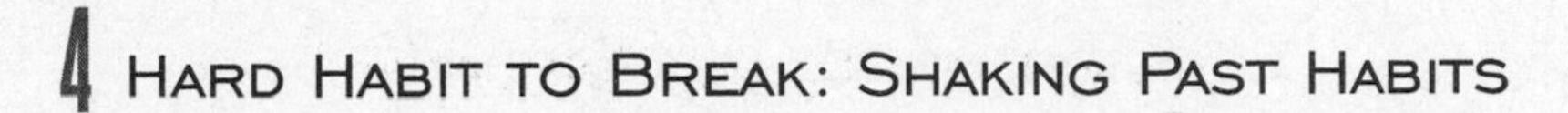

## 4 HARD HABIT TO BREAK: SHAKING PAST HABITS

1. Sometimes it's easy to mistake God's patience for approval in the way we're living. What past habits is God asking you to shake?
2. How can you use your weakness to model Christ's love to your children?
3. How do mistakes from your past affect your parenting today?
4. What things weigh heavy on your heart? How can God help you "extract" them and use them for His glory?

### Digging Deeper

**2 Corinthians 12:8–10** **Romans 2:4**
**Psalm 139:23–24** **Romans 4:7–8** **1 Corinthians 10:12–13**

## 5 FOREVER YOUNG: STRIVING FOR THE CHILDHOOD I NEVER HAD

1. What do you think are some of the longings of Gen X parents? Do you find yourself trying to give your child what you wished you had growing up?
2. Do you ever struggle with looking to tomorrow—when you can "get everything under control" and "real life can begin"?
3. How can you rejoice in your busy, crazy, jumbled days?
4. How do you live in today and enjoy your children today?

### Digging Deeper

**Romans 11:33–35** **Psalm 40:5**
**Jeremiah 29:11** **Jeremiah 33:3** **Psalm 111:10**

## 6 I'LL STAND BY YOU: PARENTING ROLES THROUGH THE AGES AND STAGES

1. What has God taught you through your role as a parent?
2. Were your parents permissive? Strict? Or did they find a healthy balance? How does the way you were parented affect your parenting?
3. Author Jen Doucette says, "In an astonishing twist of Providence, God uses the true pain of motherhood to shape us, mold us, grow us, transform us, and make us Real—more like Himself: 'Therefore we do not lose heart. Though outwardly we are wasting away, yet inwardly we are being renewed day by day' (2 Corinthians 4:16)." How has God made you more like Himself through your parenting?
4. In what ways does God want to work through you…today?

**Digging Deeper**

**Ecclesiastes 4:9–10** **Isaiah 43:2**
**1 Corinthians 1:30** **Philippians 2:13** **Hebrews 13:21**

## 7 WORDS INTO ACTION: MINDING THOUGHTS, TAMING TONGUES

1. How do you feel self-talk (the things you keep telling yourself in your mind, whether good or bad) affects your parenting?
2. How do your attitude and thoughts alter the "weather" of your home?
3. In what ways can you insure God's truth "covers" all your inner thoughts?
4. In what ways can you help your children control their thoughts and words?

**Digging Deeper**

**Psalm 15:1–3** **Proverbs 15:23**
**Proverbs 12:14** **Colossians 4:6** **1 Samuel 16:7**

## 8 ONCE IN A LIFETIME: SPENDING TIME WITH FAMILY

1. More than any other generation, Gen X parents have prioritized spending time with family. Is this true for you?

2. Do you often encounter people (e.g., bosses) who do not understand the priority you place on your time at home?

3. Do you ever have that nagging feeling that tells you what you're doing isn't enough? How do you combat that?

4. What role has God played in choosing the priorities you have?

**Digging Deeper**

**Psalm 103:1–4**   **Jeremiah 31:3**
**Psalm 63:3–5**   **Psalm 143:6–8**   **Psalm 107:43**

## 9 ADULT EDUCATION: IMPROVING PARENTING SKILLS

1. Do you ever struggle with "lazy parenting"—letting things slide because you don't want to deal with them? Why or why not?

2. In what ways has God helped your character match your assignment as a parent?

3. Do you desire altered attitudes, redeemed responses, and strength to overcome your slothful ways? If so, what's the first step to achieving these things?

4. In what ways does God hold you up on the bumpy road of life? How does knowing this keep you humble?

**Digging Deeper**

**1 Corinthians 1:30**   **1 Corinthians 4:20**
**Isaiah 50:4**   **Proverbs 18:15**   **Psalm 9:10**

## 10 AUTOMATIC MAN: MAKING ROOM FOR DADDY

1. How is the role of "dad" viewed in your home?
2. What changes do you wish you could make in this area? What does God's Word say?
3. Suppose you were to offer one of the following to your husband/wife: respect, friendship, room, praise, time, grace, and love. Which do you think he/she would desire most?
4. What steps can you take to give this gift?

### Digging Deeper

**1 Corinthians 13:1–5** **Ephesians 6:4**
**Ephesians 5:24–33** **Proverbs 5:18** **1 Peter 3:7**

## 11 HOLD ON LOOSELY: RAISING CONTENT KIDS

1. How do you teach your children contentment?
2. Do you ever have trouble with contentment yourself? Why?
3. Would you say money issues are one of the biggest struggles in your family? What does God want you to do about this?
4. Did the way you were parented affect your view of money now? How can you combat those struggles with God's Word?

### Digging Deeper

**Luke 3:14** **Philippians 4:11–13**
**Hebrews 13:5–6** **Philippians 3:8** **Matthew 6:31–34**

## 12 WHITE WEDDING: MARRIAGE MATTERS

1. In what ways do you put your marriage first? Why is this important?
2. What do you think are the biggest struggles in marriages today? Why?
3. How has divorce affected your life?
4. What is God asking you to do to strengthen your marriage?

### Digging Deeper

**Romans 14:** **Ephesians 4:31-32**
**Psalm 25:4-5** **Psalm 37:4-6** **Isaiah 43:19**

## 13 LAY YOUR HANDS ON ME: HANDS-ON PARENTING

1. How do you currently promote teamwork between family members? How can you improve on your system?
2. Jesus instructed, directed, prodded, and encouraged His disciples. What other examples did He provide in "training up" those who were under Him?
3. In what specific ways can you teach your children that hard work will result in rewards?
4. What is God's view on reaping awards?

### Digging Deeper

**Isaiah 48:17** **Ephesians 6:7**
**Galatians 5:5** **1 Corinthians 12:5** **Proverbs 12:14**

## 14 Sun Always Shines on TV: Tackling the Media Monster

1. What challenges do you face concerning the media influences in your home?
2. How did television influence your growing-up years?
3. Are your kids drawn to all things entertaining? If so, how can you make an "unseen" God as real and exciting as anything the TV offers?
4. In what ways is your lifestyle different from that of non-Christians? In what ways is it similar? What is God speaking to your heart about this?

### Digging Deeper

**Galatians 5:22** **Luke 16:15**
**1 Thessalonians 5:21** **1 John 4:1** **Titus 2:14**

## 15 All over the World: Creating a Well-Connected Neighborhood

1. How do you teach your children friendship and loyalty?
2. Do you open your home to friends and family? How has this benefited your children?
3. What type of "community" have you created for your children?
4. Is there someone, somewhere, that God wants you to bring into your community?

### Digging Deeper

**Romans 1:14** **Romans 10:14–15**
**John 3:27** **Philippians 1:9** **John 3:21**

## 16 BIG LOVE: AND THE GREATEST OF THESE IS LOVE

1. How do you show your children they're loved?
2. Do you believe that having a holy fear of God keeps us on the right track? How do you teach this "fear" to your children?
3. Why is giving consequences for wrong actions an important part of parenting? What is God speaking to you about this?

### Digging Deeper

**Deuteronomy 8:5** **Job 5:17**
**Psalm 94:12** **Hebrews 12:5-11** **Revelation 3:19**

## 17 YOU MIGHT THINK: TEACHING VALUES IN AN "ANYTHING GOES" CULTURE

1. In what ways do you work at building your children's moral character?
2. So how *do* you teach values in an "anything goes" culture?
3. What part of "anything goes" bothers you the most?
4. How can you be a "holy experiment" for God? What is He asking you to do?

### Digging Deeper

**Isaiah 54:13** **Acts 16:31**
**Proverbs 22:6** **Isaiah 44:3** **Isaiah 65:23**

## 18 1-2-3-4: COUNTING ON EDUCATION

1. What educational convictions do you have concerning your children?
2. Would you describe yourself as a helicopter parent? A stealth fighter parent? Something else?
3. Why do you want your children to excel? To see their name on the honor roll? To ensure they get into the best colleges? As a bragging point to grandparents? Other?
4. What is God speaking to your heart concerning your children's education?

### Digging Deeper

**James 3:17** **James 1:5**
**Philippians 3:8-12** **Proverbs 2:6** **Isaiah 11:2-3**

## 19 BE GOOD TO YOURSELF: TAKING CARE OF GOALS AND DREAMS

1. Do you think it's important for parents to strive for goals and dreams? Why or why not?
2. What dreams has God placed on your heart?
3. Is it possible to balance parenting and following your dreams? Why or why not?
4. What benefits will your children receive by having parents who follow their dreams?

### Digging Deeper

**2 Timothy 4:7-8** **1 Corinthians 13:12**
**1 Corinthians 15:10** **2 Thessalonians 1:11** **Psalm 63:8**

## 20 DANGER ZONE: ORGANIZED ACTIVITIES—HOW MUCH IS TOO MUCH?

1. How do you decide how many activities to sign your kids up for?
2. Do you feel you've achieved a healthy balance?
3. Have you ever felt you've "exploited" your kids to follow your "dream" for them? In what way?
4. Have you discovered your child's unique shape? What does your child enjoy the most?

### Digging Deeper

**Ephesians 1:18** **Ephesians 5:10**
**Ephesians 5:17** **Galatians 5:22–23** **2 Timothy 3:16**

## 21 IN MY DREAMS: TO COMPARE OR NOT COMPARE

1. Do you ever compare yourself to other parents? How does this affect you?
2. Do you ever find yourself being judged by someone else's criteria? How do you respond to those comparisons?
3. Have you ever missed out on enjoying friends, family, and life in general because you were too busy comparing yourself to others?
4. What does God's Word say about comparisons? What is He speaking to your heart?

### Digging Deeper

**Luke 18:11** **2 Corinthians 1:12**
**Psalm 43:5** **Amos 7:14** **Romans 12:16**

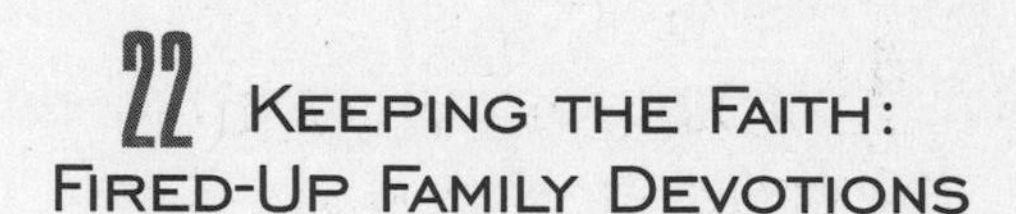

## 22 Keeping the Faith: Fired-Up Family Devotions

1. What are your successes or struggles concerning family devotions?
2. Do you have any fears about studying the Bible with your children? What are they?
3. What should you do if your spouse doesn't want to participate in family devotions?
4. Why is it important to consider every aspect of our lives in relation to God's Word? How can you help your children do this?

### Digging Deeper

**Luke 1:50** **Isaiah 57:15**
**Ephesians 5:1–2** **1 Timothy 4:12** **1 Chronicles 28:9**

## 23 I Wanna Break Free: Freeing Your Children from the World's Idols

1. How do you teach your kids where true satisfaction is found? Why is this important?
2. What idols do you feel kids struggle with in this day and age?
3. Why are we, as parents, caught up with the world's idols? More important, how can we keep our kids from falling into this trap?

### Digging Deeper

**Romans 6:13** **2 Kings 17:41**
**Psalm 84:2** **Jeremiah 1:16** **Acts 17:22–24**

## 24 CAUGHT UP IN YOU: GETTING FILLED WITH GOD

1. Children are drawn to God by parents who have a real relationship with the Lord. How do you model this relationship?
2. What struggles do you have in this area?
3. What does it look like to be long-necked and widemouthed, open to God's filling? How can you do this in your life…today?

**Digging Deeper**

**Numbers 23:19** **1 Timothy 6:17**
**Psalm 107:9** **Psalm 34:10** **Isaiah 55:1–3**

## 25 LIVIN' ON A PRAYER: PRAYER CHANGES THINGS

1. Can you think of an incident in which you personally recognized how much courage parenting takes?
2. From the example of Joshua, where do we find our courage and strength?
3. When have you experienced an answer to prayer that wasn't exactly what you hoped for? Did God show His faithfulness despite your disappointment?
4. How can you prepare your heart to receive God's answers?
5. How has prayer changed things in your life…or changed you?

**Digging Deeper**

**Isaiah 40:29–31** **Colossians 1:11**
**1 Kings 8:21–23** **Jeremiah 42:3** **Philippians 1:3–7**

## 26 FAITH: FAITH, NOT FEAR

1. Have you ever experienced a time of intense fear? How did God use that to draw you closer to Him?
2. What are some things that cause you to fear for your children? Why?
3. Who ultimately has control? How should this affect the way you speak, think, and act—especially around your children?
4. How do God's promises help you overcome fear?

### Digging Deeper

**Romans 4:20–22** **Isaiah 26:3–4**
**2 Corinthians 4:18** **Romans 15:13** **Hebrews 11:6**

## GOOD-BYE

1. What hopes do you have for Gen Xers as parents?
2. How do you feel about our calling as Gen Xers?
3. Do you agree that Gen X *can* symbolize "Generation Christ"? How does this encourage you?
4. What mark are you leaving for your children to follow? How will this lead them to Christ?

### Digging Deeper

**Proverbs 4:13** **Isaiah 55:3**
**John 14:21** **1 John 5:1–3** **Revelation 22:14**

# Acknowledgments

John, my parenting partner for love and life. Your encouragement, wisdom, and dedication to our family make this journey a joy.

Cory, Leslie, and Nathan. Thanks for giving me plenty of material to write about, and thank you for loving your mom. You are growing to be wonderful, godly young people.

My Grandma Dolores. May the heritage of your faith continue through the years.

My mom and dad, Linda Martin and Ron Waddell. For all the years of loving me.

My mother and father-in-law, John and Darlyne Goyer. John is a great dad because of your wonderful example.

My heart-friends who encouraged me always: Joanna, Twyla, Tara, and Cindy and Kayleigh.

My prayer friends from One Heart, AWSA, Blessed Hope and the Coeur d'Alene gals. Your prayers strengthen me.

My agent, Janet Kobobel Grant, who believes in my ideas and cheers me on.

My editor, Steffany Woolsey, and the Multnomah team. I thank God for you!

Finally, this book wouldn't be possible without the amazing Gen X parents who offered their prayers, quotes, and input on the manuscript! (Especially Cara, Allison, Amy, Ocieanna, Michelle, and Jeanette, who gave a TON of help and input.)

Care Barndt
Scott Barndt
Abbey Bruner
Heidi Burns
Craig Chatriand
Koryn Chatriand
Stephanie Clancy
Tiffany Colter
Gina Conroy
Caryn Dahm
Melanie Lee Dickerson
Robert Dickson
Michelle Dickson
Heather Donnelli
Julie Ellsworth
Judy Fedele
Andrea Fields
Ocieanna Fleiss
Tanya Flores
Debby Gardner
Joey Gardner
Heather Graf
Rebecca Haram
Shannon Hassler
Andora Henson
Jessica Holst
Jeanette Hanscome
Kristy Hatfield
Michelle Hortenberry
Michelle Hutchinson
Jennifer Hruska
Lisa Jackson
Elizabeth Johnson
Jenna Jospehson
Fran Korpela
Brenda Lacey
Mona Marushak
Gina Meekma
Angela Meuser
Dani Meyers
Robin Miller
Wendy Park
Lezlie Northagen
Amy Parker
Lisa Peck
Randall Peck
Tanya Peila
Mollie Philbin
Cara Putman
Jennifer Riale
Dee Rockman
Jennifer Rudnick
Thresa Saenz
Patricia Sawyer
Carrie Seberger
Katie Schnee
Kristi Siler
Lauri Smit
Amy Steele
Beth Tankersley
Kelli Theobald
Doug Tooke
Amy Wallace
Rich Waltman
Jeanette Waltman
Andrena Willett
Allison Wilson
Michelle Wheatley
Bill Wyatt
Cheryl Wyatt

. . . and many more who prayed and cheered me on!

# NOTES


1. William Strauss and Neil Howe, *Generations: The History of America's Future, 1594 to 2069* (New York: William Morrow and Company, 1991), 64.
2. Graeme Codrington and Sue Grant-Marshall, *Mind the Gap!* (London: Penguin Publishers, 2005), 13.
3. Codrington and Grant-Marshall, *Mind the Gap*, 1.
4. Ibid., 253.
5. From Biblesoft's *New Exhaustive Strong's Numbers and Concordance with Expanded Greek-Hebrew Dictionary* (Biblesoft and International Bible Translators, 1994).
6. Codrington and Grant-Marshall, *Mind the Gap*, 92.
7. Gregory A. Boyd, *Seeing Is Believing* (Grand Rapids, MI: Baker Books, 2004), 22–23.
8. From Biblesoft's *New Exhaustive Strong's Numbers and Concordance with Expanded Greek-Hebrew Dictionary* (Biblesoft and International Bible Translators, 1994).
9. Wesley L. Duewel, *Let God Guide You Daily* (Grand Rapids, MI: Zondervan, 1985), 45.
10. Oswald Chambers, *My Utmost for His Highest* (Grand Rapids, MI: Discovery House Publishers, 1992), November 14 entry.
11. Codrington and Grant-Marshall, *Mind the Gap*, 10.
12. Dr. Rick and Kathy Hicks, *Boomers, Xers, and Other Strangers: Understanding the Generational Differences That Divide Us* (Wheaton, IL: Tyndale House Publishers, 1999), 185.
13. Bartleby.com, "Bernard of Clairvaux, Saint," http://www.bartleby.com/65/be/BernardCSt.html (accessed May 4, 2006).
14. From Biblesoft's *New Exhaustive Strong's Numbers and Concordance with Expanded Greek-Hebrew Dictionary* (Biblesoft and International Bible Translators, 1994).
15. Max Lucado, *Give It All To Him: A Story of New Beginnings* (Nashville, TN: W Publishing Group), 11–12.
16. Ibid., 30–31.
17. Chambers, *My Utmost for His Highest*, June 23 entry.
18. From Biblesoft's *New Exhaustive Strong's Numbers and Concordance with Expanded Greek-Hebrew Dictionary* (Biblesoft and International Bible Translators, 1994).
19. Codrington and Grant-Marshall, *Mind the Gap*, 74.
20. Donna Partow, *Standing Firm* (Minneapolis, MN: Bethany House, 2001), 18.
21. John Fischer, *Finding God Where You Least Expect Him* (Eugene, OR: Harvest House Publishers, 2003), 12.
22. Codrington and Grant-Marshall, *Mind the Gap*, 75.
23. Michaele Birney Arneson, "Parents Today Part II," *TD Monthly*, June 2005, http://www.toydirectory.com/monthly/article.asp?id=1329 (accessed May 4, 2006).
24. From Biblesoft's *New Exhaustive Strong's Numbers and Concordance with Expanded Greek-Hebrew Dictionary* (Biblesoft and International Bible Translators, 1994).

25. E. M. Bounds, *Power Through Prayer* (Omaha, Nebraska: Quick Verse, 2005), 1.
26. Chambers, *My Utmost for His Highest*, April 18 entry.
27. Codrington and Grant-Marshall, *Mind the Gap*, 17.
28. Jenn Doucette, *The Velveteen Mommy* (Colorado Springs, CO: NavPress, 2005), 13, 15.
29. Tedd Tripp, *Shepherding a Child's Heart* (Wapwallopen, PA: Shepherd Press, 1995), xxi.
30. Codrington and Grant-Marshall, *Mind the Gap*, 39, 49.
31. Wesley L. Duewel, *Let God Guide You Daily* (Grand Rapids, MI: Zondervan, 1988), 45.
32. Answers in Genesis, "Blaise Pascal," http://www.answersingenesis.org/docs/314.asp (accessed May 4, 2006).
33. Codrington and Grant-Marshall, *Mind the Gap*, 94–95.
34. Graeme Codrington, "Generation X Papers: 25 Sentences That Define a Generation," taken from his honors thesis on Generation X, 1998, http://www.tomorrowtoday.biz/generations/xpaper1010.htm (accessed May 4, 2006).
35. From Biblesoft's *New Exhaustive Strong's Numbers and Concordance with Expanded Greek-Hebrew Dictionary* (Biblesoft and International Bible Translators, 1994).
36. Ibid.
37. Robert Benson, *Living Prayer* (New York: Penguin Putnam, 1998), 27.
38. Ibid., 24.
39. Kenneth Copley, *The Great Deceiver: Unmasking the Lies of Satan* (Chicago, IL: Moody Publishing, 2001), 94–95.
40. Karen E. Klein, "The ABCs of Selling to Generation X," *Business Week Online*, April 15, 2004, http://www.businessweek.com/smallbiz/content/apr2004/sb20040414_0567_sb001.htm (accessed May 4, 2006).
41. Meg Grant, "Funny Girl," *Reader's Digest*, September 2005: 87–88.
42. Klein, "The ABCs of Selling to Generation X" (accessed May 4, 2006).
43. *Ryrie Study Bible*, NAS (Chicago, Illinois: Moody Publishing, 1985) , note on Hosea 2:19.
44. Charles S. Spurgeon, *All of Grace* (Hiawatha, Iowa: Parsons Technology, Inc., 1997), Electronic Edition STEP Files.
45. Lisa Whelchel, *Speaking Mom-ese* (Brentwood, TN: Integrity Publishers, 2005), 81
46. Ibid., 84.
47. Codrington and Grant-Marshall, *Mind the Gap*, 54.
48. Chambers, *My Utmost for His Highest*, November 11 entry.
49. Joyce Meyer, *How to Succeed at Being Yourself* (Cincinnati, OH: Harrison House, 1999), 36.
50. Henry Blackaby, *Experiencing God Workbook* (Nashville, TN: Lifeway Press, 1990), 39.
51. Kent Crockett, *Making Today Count for Eternity* (Sisters, OR: Multnomah, 2001), 123.
52. From Biblesoft's *New Exhaustive Strong's Numbers and Concordance with Expanded Greek-Hebrew Dictionary* (Biblesoft and International Bible Translators, 1994).
53. Steven L. Case, *The Book of Uncommon Prayer* (Grand Rapids, MI: Youth Specialties, 2002), 99.
54. Codrington and Grant-Marshall, *Mind the Gap*, 274.

55. Ibid., 13.
56. Hicks, *Boomers, Xers, and Other Strangers*, 301.
57. Klein, "The ABCs of Selling to Generation X," (accessed May 4, 2006).
58. Robert Benson, *A Good Life* (Brewster, MA: Paraclete Press), 33.
59. Ibid., 128.
60. Chambers, *My Utmost for His Highest*, June 17 entry.
61. Caroline Overington, "Gen X Keen on the ABCs of Raising Gen Y," *The Age Online*, July 24, 2004, http://www.reachadvisors.com/agearticle.html (accessed May 4, 2006).
62. Myron A. Marty, *Decades of Discord: Daly Life in the United States 1960–1990* (Westport, CT: Greenwood Press, 1997), 185.
63. Victor Bondi, ed., *American Decades 1980–1989* (Detroit, MI: Gale Research, 1996), 146, as quoted in Hicks, *Boomers, Xers, and Other Strangers*, 179.
64. Hicks, *Boomers, Xers, and Other Strangers*, 297.
65. Klein, "The ABCs of Selling to Generation X," (accessed May 4, 2006).
66. Ibid.
67. "The Motherhood Study" (New York: The Motherhood Project, Institute for American Values), 8.
68. Larry Burkett, *Great Is Thy Faithfulness* (Uhrichsville, OH: Promise Press), July 7.
69. From Biblesoft's *New Exhaustive Strong's Numbers and Concordance with Expanded Greek-Hebrew Dictionary* (Biblesoft and International Bible Translators, 1994).
70. Tripp, *Shepherding a Child's Heart*, 45–46.
71. Tim LaHaye, Jerry B. Jenkins, and Frank M. Martin, *Embracing Eternity* (Omaha, NE: Quickverse), April 24 entry.
72. Codrington and Grant-Marshall, *Mind the Gap*, 91.
73. Lynne C. Lancaster and David Stillman, *When Generations Collide: Who They Are. Why They Clash: How to Solve the Generational Puzzle at Work* (New York: HarperCollins Publishers, 2003), 115.
74. Hicks, *Boomers, Xers, and Other Strangers*, 293.
75. David Athens, "Gen X Hits Big 4-0," *Post-Trib.Com*, July 19, 2005, http://www.iun.edu/~newsnw/articles/07-19-05_post_trib.pdf (accessed May 4, 2006).
76. Lois and Alan Gordon, *The Columbia Chronicles of American Life 1910–1992* (New York: Columbia University Press, 1995), 672, as quoted in Hicks, *Boomers, Xers, and Other Strangers*, 179.
77. Myron A. Marty, *Decades of Discord* (Westport, CT: Greenwood Press, 1997), p. 207.
78. Jim Killam, "A Match Made in Hollywood," *Marriage Partnership*, Winter 1999, http://www.christianitytoday.com/mp/9m4/9m4026.html (accessed May 4, 2006).
79. Michaele Birney Arneson, "Parents Today Part II" (accessed May 4, 2006).
80. Codrington and Grant-Marshall, *Mind the Gap*, 96.
81. *God's Words of Life for Leaders* (Grand Rapids, MI: Zondervan, 1999), 164–65.
82. Donna Partow, *Standing Firm* (Minneapolis, MN: Bethany House, 2001), 17.
83. Zig Ziglar, *See You at the Top: Daily Motivational Thoughts from Zig Ziglar* (Bloomington, MN: Garbort's, Inc., 1999), January 14 entry.

84. Hicks, *Boomers, Xers, and Other Strangers*, 41.
85. Enola G. Aird, Christopher E. Barnes, Barbara Clinton, et al., *God's Word of Life for Leaders* (Grand Rapids, MI: Zondervan, 1999) 50.
86. Codrington and Grant-Marshall, *Mind the Gap*, 50.
87. Marty, *Decades of Discord*, 205.
88. Enola G. Aird, Christopher E. Barnes, Barbara Clinton, et al., *The Motherhood Study* (New York: The Motherhood Project, Institute for American Values), 8.
89. Boyd, *Seeing Is Believing*, 12–13.
90. Hicks, *Boomers, Xers, and Other Strangers*, 32.
91. Mike Yaconelli, "Ten Easy Steps to Guarantee a Successful Youth Ministry," *Youth Specialties Online*, http://www.youthspecialties.com/articles/Yaconelli/easysteps.php?printIt=yes (accessed May 4, 2006).
92. Enola G. Aird, Christopher E. Barnes, Barbara Clinton, et al., *God's Words of Life for Leaders* (Grand Rapids, MI: Zondervan, 1999), 195.
93. Fischer, *Finding God Where You Least Expect Him*, 16.
94. Codrington and Grant-Marshall, *Mind the Gap*, 50.
95. George Barna, *Generation Next: What You Need to Know About Today's Youth* (Ventura, CA: Regal, 1995), 24, as quoted in Hicks, *Boomers, Xers, and Other Strangers*, 265.
96. Bondi, ed., *American Decades 1980–1989*, 185–86.
97. From Biblesoft's *New Exhaustive Strong's Numbers and Concordance with Expanded Greek Hebrew Dictionary* (Biblesoft and International Bible Translators, 1994).
98. Robert Wolgemuth, *The Most Important Place on Earth* (Nashville, TN: Thomas Nelson Books), 194–95.
99. Henry Blackaby and Melvin Blackaby, *Experiencing God Together* (Nashville, TN: Broadman and Holman Publishers), 9.
100. Ibid., 11.
101. Ibid., 6.
102. Marty, *Decades of Discord*, 244.
103. Doucette, *Velveteen Mommy*, 13.
104. Codrington, "Generation X Papers," (accessed May 4, 2006).
105. Henry and Melvin Blackaby, *Experiencing God Together*, xiii.
106. Codrington and Grant-Marshall, *Mind the Gap*, 86–87.
107. Wolgemuth, *The Most Important Place on Earth*, 180.
108. Ibid., 170.
109. Gary Smalley and John Trent, *The Blessing* (Nashville, TN: Thomas Nelson Books), 59, 56.
110. Lancaster and Stillman, *When Generations Collide*, 24.
111. From Biblesoft's *New Exhaustive Strong's Numbers and Concordance with Expanded Greek Hebrew Dictionary* (Biblesoft and International Bible Translators, 1994).
112. Hicks, *Boomers, Xers, and Other Strangers*, 12.
113. *God's Word of Life for Leaders*, 89–90.

114. Chambers, *My Utmost for His Highest,* June 13 entry.

115. Strauss and Howe, *Generations,* 322.

116. *God's Word of Life for Leaders,* 204.

117. Lancaster and Stillman, *When Generations Collide,* 255.

118. Codrington and Grant-Marshall, *Mind the Gap,* 90.

119. Daniel Scarpinato, "Gen X Parents Putting Tighter Rein on Schools" *Arizona Daily Star,* October 16, 2005, http://www.azstarnet.com/dailystar/news/98017.php (accessed May 4, 2006).

120. Ibid.

121. Lancaster and Stillman, *When Generations Collide,* 100–110.

122. Michaele Birney Arneson, "Parents Today Part II" (accessed May 4, 2006).

123. Codrington and Grant-Marshall, *Mind the Gap,* 158.

124. Jerry Bridges, *The Practice of Godliness* (Colorado Springs, CO: NavPress, 2001), 93.

125. Chambers, *My Utmost for His Highest,* November 10 entry.

126. Bette Davis, *The Lonely Life,* 1962; quotation #1772 from *Laura Moncur's Motivational Quotations,* http://www.quotationspage.com/quote/1772.html (accessed May 4, 2006).

127. William Strauss and Neil Howe, *The Fourth Turning* (New York: Broadway Books), 327.

128. Ibid., 328.

129. From Biblesoft's *New Exhaustive Strong's Numbers and Concordance with Expanded Greek-Hebrew Dictionary* (Biblesoft and International Bible Translators, 1994).

130. Timothy Jones, *Nurturing a Child's Soul* (Nashville, TN: Word Publishing), 21.

131. Hicks, *Boomers, Xers, and Other Strangers,* 18.

132. The Monks of New Skete, *Rise Up with a Listening Heart* (New York: Yorkville Press, 2004), 37.

133. Neil Anderson and Robert Saucy, *The Common Made Holy* (Eugene, OR: Harvest House Publishers, 1997).

134. William Strauss and Neil Howe, *Millennials Rising* (New York: Vintage Books, 2000), 366.

135. *Nelson Study Bible* (Cedar Rapids, IA: Parsons Technology, Inc., 1997), Electronic Edition STEP Files.

136. Codrington and Grant-Marshall, *Mind the Gap,* 233.

137. Ibid., 245.

138. Tony Evans, *The Fire That Ignites* (Sisters, OR: Multnomah Publishers, 2003), 63.

139. Lou Priolo, *Teach Them Diligently: How to Use the Scriptures in Child Training* (Woodruff, SC: Timeless Texts, 2000), 156–57.

140. Codrington and Grant-Marshall, *Mind the Gap,* 20.

141. *The Handbook of Bible Application* (Wheaton, IL: Tyndale House Publishers).

142. Boyd, *Seeing Is Believing,* 150.

143. Richard and Renee Durfield, *Raising Pure Kids in an Impure World* (Minneapolis, MN: Bethany House, 2004), 19–20.

144. Fischer, *Finding God Where You Least Expect Him,* 33.

145. Marty, *Decades of Discord,* 230.

146. Bondi, ed., *American Decades 1980–1989,* 184–85.

147. Hicks, *Boomers, Xers, and Other Strangers,* 186.
148. A. W. Tozer, *Whatever Happened to Worship?* (Authentic Lifestyle, 1997), 28-29.
149. Chambers, *My Utmost for His Highest,* January 7 entry.
150. George Gallup Jr., *The Next American Spirituality* (Colorado Springs, CO: Cook Communications, 2000), 25.
151. Chambers, *My Utmost for His Highest,* 26.
152. Dr. Tim Kimmel, *Grace Based Parenting* (Nashville, TN: W Publishing, 2004), 108–109.
153. Hicks, *Boomers, Xers, and Other Strangers,* 219.
154. Bondi, ed., *American Decades 1980–1989,* 180.
155. Teresa Whitehurst, *How Would Jesus Raise a Child?* (Grand Rapids, MI: Baker Books, 2003), page 116–7.
156. John Fischer, *Fearless Faith* (Eugene, OR: Harvest House Publishers, 2002), 8.
157. Hicks, *Boomers, Xers, and Other Strangers,* 254.